Maharshi Dayanand Saraswati Book Series-25

The Sāṅkyha Darśana

The Knowledge of Embodiment and Disembodiment of the Soul

(Sanskrit Text, Roman Transliteration and English Commentary)

Prof. Ravi Prakash Arya
Chair Professor
Maharshi Dayanand Saraswati Chair (UGC)
Maharshi Dayanand University, Haryana

Assisted by
Alois Heinrich

Amazon Books, USA
In Association with
Indian Foundation for Vedic Science
1051, Sector-1, Rohtak, Haryana, India
Ph. 09313033917; 9650183२60
Email: vedicscience@rediffmail.com; vedicscience@gmail.com
Web: https://vedic-sciences.com

First Edition

Kali era 5126 (c. 2024)
Kalpa era 1,97,29,49,126
Brahma era 15,55,21,97,29,49,126

ISBN: 978-93-94724-69-3

© Author

Printed by

Indian Foundation for Vedic Science, 1051, Sector-1, Rohtak-124001, Haryana

Contents

Preface

Six philosophical thoughts, most often called as Ṣaḍ Darśanas of ancient India, are the help books to understand the different aspects of the comprehensive knowledge enshrined in the Vedas. These six Darśanas are not different from Vedas but are part and parcel of the long Vedic tradition of India. That is why these books are called Āstika (theistic) Darśanas, as they follow Vedas as authority. The philosophical thoughts developed other than these were called as Nāstika Darśanas, or those developed disregarding the guidelines of the Vedas. The terms Āstika and Nāstika denote admitting the authority of the Veda and discarding the same.

All six philosophical schools supplement each other. They deal with separate aspects of knowledge and creation. For instance, the Mīmānsā of Jaminī deals with karmakāṇḍa. Karmakāṇḍa represents creation as the karma of Brahman and karmas to be done by human beings for their pārmārthika (spiritual) elevation and laukika (material) upliftment and advancement. Thus, karmakāṇḍa of Mimānsā, on one side, deals with karmas that produce sāttvika sanskāras leading an individual towards divinity; on the other hand, it talks about the sankāras of material things for devising eco-friendly technologies for upliftment and advancement of human life at the laukika (mundane) level.

The Nyāya of Gautama deals with research methodology. It teaches all methods and techniques through which humans can attain true knowledge of material things, the cosmos, and Brahman.

The Vedānta of Vyasa deals with the supreme entity Brahman, the Nimitta Kāraṇa (efficient cause) of the whole creation and the Governor of the universe in the manifest and unmanifest state. This whole universe is governed by certain rules, which are nothing but the will of Brahman reflected as information in His cosmic mind called Prakṛti. This will of Brahman is also called a unified law or Ṛta, which is at work in the existing universe in diverse forms.

The Vaiśeṣika of Kaṇāda deals with the physics and metaphysics of the existing universe. It divides padārthas (all entities of the visible and invisible world) into six categories: dravya (material and spiritual entity), guṇa (quality), karma (action/motion), sāmānya (generality), viśeṣa (individuality), and samavāya (inherence).

It explains and describes guṇa-dharmas (properties) of all six padārthas. When applied for beneficial use, knowledge of the properties of these padārthas (entities of the visible and invisible world) empowers us to improve the conditions of our mundane lives. The same understanding of the properties of material entities makes us realise their temporariness. It inspires us to self-realise and realise Brahman called Mokṣa, the prime objective of human life.

The Yogadarśana of Patañjali is a practical book that deals with the method of disembodiment of the soul. Its main objective is to help humans develop themselves to the extent of realising the Supreme Power/God.

The Yoga is a science of psycho-engineering. It provides all the tools and techniques to engineer the human mind so that an individual being may be elevated to divinity. It reveals the secrets of life, death and mokṣa. Just as physical sciences and technologies involve kinetic and potential energies for their operation; similarly, the science of psycho-engineering and māntrika technology developed in ancient India was based on Bhāvanā Sanskāra or psychic energy of Vaśeṣika tradition. The Yogadarśana teaches us how to pool the psychic energy and utilise it in achieving various siddhis or divine powers. Yoga enables one to command over one's mental functions or processes and develop one's full potential.

Sāṅkhya and Creation

Generally, scholars think that the Sāṅkhya Darśana deals with the creation of the universe. Nevertheless, the creation of the universe is not the primary subject of Sāṅkhya. The Sāṅkhya Darśana primarily deals with the embodiment of an individual soul. It explains the existence of Prakṛti and Puruṣa [soul] and their various characteristics. It also beautifully describes the body's production from Prakṛti. In addition, it explains the purpose of creation.

It also discusses in depth the purpose of the origin of the body, the thirteen senses and tanmātras. Two types of bodies and the soul's journey in different species have been explained remarkably. Having explained self-realisation technically [from the point of Śāstra], the means of self-realisation are described within the ambit of Śāstra through famous examples prevalent in society.

It also discusses certain other issues related to or unrelated to self-realisation that can be contrary to the fundamental principles of Sāṅkhya.

According to the Sāṅkhya, Viveka [discrimination between Soul and body] leads to apavarga [self-realisation].

However, we can indirectly infer the process of physical creation as per Sāṅkhya.

As per Sāṅkhya, ahaṅkāra from the point of sattva, rajas and tamas guṇas is of three types—Taijas Ahaṅkāra, Vaikārika Ahaṅkāra and Bhūtādi Ahaṅkāra.

(1). From Taijas ahaṅkāra proceed mind, five sensory organs.

(2). From Vaikārika ahaṅkāra proceed motor organs.

(3). From Bhūtādi ahaṅkāra proceed five bhūta [matter] tanmātras [sensations], and from five Bhūta [matter] tanmātras proceed active matter particles [electrons, protons and neutrons] forming five gross elements [representing five states of matter].

According to Sāṅkhya prakṛi has two forms—sat and asat. However, prakṛti is the same irrespective of its two forms.

समानः प्रकृतेर्द्वयोः ॥ ३४ ॥

samānaḥ prakṛterdvayoḥ ॥ 34॥

[Meaning 1] (dvayoḥ) Between two —soul and Prakṛti, (samānaḥ) it is proper to accept (prakṛteḥ) Prakṛti as the material cause of the bodies of souls or creation.

[Meaning 2] Prakṛti has two forms—sat and asat. In the form of sat, it is eternal, but in the form of asat, it continues to change. In its causal form, Prakṛti is sat, and in its product form, Prakṛti is asta. The sūtra says that (prakṛteḥ) Prakṛti is (samānam) the same irrespective of its (dvayoḥ) two forms.

In its sat form, the three guṇas are in a balanced state or remain inactive, but in its asat form, the three guṇas are imbalanced and become active. These three guṇas of Sāṅkhya have three different properties— sattva has the property of rāga [attraction], rajas have the property of virāga [repulson], and tamas has the property of neutrality. These three guṇas — sattva, rajas and tamas are operative in three material particles called electrons, protons, and neutrons.

Due to the above-cited fundamental properties of sattva, rajas and tamas guṇas, particles also have the tendency of attraction-repulsion [electrons and protons] and neutrality [neutrons].

Sāṅkhya also says that prakṛti [energy], being insentient [jaḍa], cannot be active until and unless it is activated by some external chetana [sentient] force called Brahman.

Does Sāṅkhya believe in God?

A lengthy discussion has been done on the existence of Ātmā [the soul] as an independent entity other than Prakṛti. According to Sāṅkhya, there are multiple souls. It differentiates between the soul and Brahman. There are many controversies rumoured by pseudo-scholars and neo-Sāṅkhyas about the Sāṅkhya Darśana that it does not accept the existence of Īśvara. This is all absurd and shows that such scholars do not know the a,b,c of Sāṅkhya. The study of Sāṅkhya informs us that Sāṅkhya never denies the existence of Īśvara. Sāṅkhya's Īśvara is the efficient cause of the creation and not the material cause, as Īśvara is not qualified to be the material cause of the creation. A material cause must have the quality to undergo the change. The Brahman and soul are both unchangeable, void of properties and eternal. They cannot undergo the change. Prakṛti has the quality of change and is made of the properties of sattva, rajas and tamas, so it is accepted as the material cause of creation.

While deliberating upon the nature of pratyakṣa pramāṇa [sensory perception], Maharṣi Kapila clearly admits the existence of Īśvara, being proved by yogic perception. According to him, sensory perception includes both—internal and external perception. The existence of Īśvara can be proved by internal perception, which can be had only by high-profile yogis. He defines pratyakṣa (sensory perception) as:

यत्संबद्धंसत्तदाकारोल्लेखि विज्ञानं तत् प्रत्यक्षम् ॥ ५४ ॥

yatsambaddham sattadākārollekhi vijñānam tatpratyakṣam ॥ 54

(pratyakṣam) Pratyakṣa [perception] is (tat) that (vijñānam) knowledge (yet) which results (sat sambaddham) from the right connection of sense organs with the external objects and (tadākārollekhi) portrays their exact form.

When this definition of pratyakṣa was called faulty, as it did not extend to the pratyakṣa of the yogīs, who can perceive past and future things. To this, Maharṣi Kapila replied as follows:

योगिनामबाह्यप्रत्यक्षत्वान्न दोषः ॥ ५५ ॥

yogināma-bāhya-pratyakṣatvānna doṣaḥ ॥ 55॥

(na doṣaḥ) There is no fault in this definition (yoginām abāhya-pratyasatvāt) because the perception of yogīs is not an external one. The perception of yogīs is an internal one. So, here, the term pratyakṣa [perception] stands for both external and internal pratyakṣa [perception].

लीनवस्तुलब्धातिशयसंबन्धाद्वाऽदोषः ॥ ५६ ॥

līna vastu labdhātiśayasaṁbandhādvādoṣaḥ ॥ 56 ॥

(vā adoṣaḥ) Or there is no fault in this definition because yogīs, through the great power of yoga, are able (labdhātiśaya-sambandha) to establish close connections with (līna vastu) things hidden in their material cause or intervened by time, distance and another object. We may call it yogic pratyakṣa.

Further, it is emphasised that for want of yogic pratyakṣa, the existence of Īśvara cannot be proved.

ईश्वरासिद्धेः ॥ ५७ ॥

īśvarāsiddheḥ ॥ 57 ॥

[First Meaning] Had the Yogic pratyakṣa not been included in the definition of pratyakṣa, (Īśvara-asiddheḥ) existence of Īśvara would not have been proved by pratyakṣa pramāṇa. Yogic pratyakṣa rules out the non-existence of Īśvara since the yogīs can have a perception of Īśvara through samādhi.

Here, a seeker can raise doubt about why we should not accept Īśvara as the material cause of the creation and discard the existence of prakṛti as the material cause. To this, the reply can be given through the second meaning of the sūtra.

[Second Meaning] (Īśvara-asiddheḥ) Īśvara cannot be established as the material cause of the world. He is the efficient cause of the world. For example, potter is the efficient cause of the pot, whereas clay is the material cause of the pot. Like the potter, Īśvara is the efficient cause; like clay, prakṛti is the material cause of creation.

From the above sūtra, it is crystal clear that Sāṅkhya admits the existence of Īśvara but does not admit Him to be the material cause of the world.

How can he be not proved as the material cause of the creation?

मुक्तबद्धयोरन्यतराभावान्न तत्सिद्धिः ॥ ५८ ॥

muktabaddhayoranyatarābhāvānna tatsiddhiḥ ॥ *58* ॥

[First meaning] (na tat siddhiḥ) Proof of Īśvara as the material cause of the world cannot be established because He is (anyatarābhāt) different from (muktabaddhayoḥ) both liberated and bonded souls.

He is neither liberated nor bonded. Had he been liberated or bonded, we could have said that decreation is caused under His liberation and creation is caused under His bondage. However, in the case of His being liberated, He would not undergo the change required for creation; in the case of His being bonded, He cannot attain the status of Īśvara being connected with dharma or adharma.

The argument that Īśvara can be taken as both a liberated and bonded soul is also refuted.

उभयथाप्यसत्करत्वम् ॥ ५९ ॥

ubhayathāpyasatkaratvam ॥ *59* ॥

(ubhayathā ap) Should we take Īśvara both for liberated or bonded? Even then, He cannot be proved as a material cause. In both the conditions [liberated and bonded], he will be a chetana sattā [sentient entity] and (asatkaratvam) chetana [sentient] cannot convert/transform or manifest itself into achetana [insentient], as this material creation is achetana [insentient].

From the preceding discussion, it is crystal clear that

the Sāṅkhya sūtras used by some innocent scholars to disapprove of the non-existence of Iśvara clearly prove His existence as an efficient cause but not as a material cause.

Maharṣi Kapila beautifully answers all the questions confronting any seeker of spirituality from birth, death till mokṣa. Sāṅkhya deals both with embodiment [bondage] and disembodiment [liberation] of the soul.

At another place, replying to the question as to who knows about the leftover sanskāras of the souls, and how their embodiment is monitored, the existence of Iśvara is directly accepted as all-knower, creator and governor.

स हि सर्ववित्सर्वकर्ता ॥ ५६ ॥

sa hi sarvavitsarvakartā ॥ *56* ॥

It all is monitored by Iśvara [God], (hi) because (saḥ) Iśvara [God] (sarvavit) knows everything [omniscient], (sarvakartā) and creator all. He monitors things accordingly.

ईदृशेश्वरसिद्धिः सिद्धा ॥ ५७ ॥

īdṛśeśvarasiddhiḥ siddhā ॥ *57* ॥

(idṛśa-Iśvara-siddhiḥ) Thus, the existence of an omniscient, all-creator and controller God (siddhā) is established.

Thus, the preceding discussion is a befitting reply to those ignorant scholars who believe that Sāṅkhya does not accept the existence of Iśvara [nirīśvara Sāṅkhya].

Sāṅkhya as Jñāna

In the Bhagavad Gītā, the Sāṅkhya Darśana is called Jñāna, and the Yogadarśana is called Karma.

लोकेऽस्मिन् द्विविधा निष्ठा पुरा प्रोक्ता मयानघ ।
ज्ञानयोगेन साङ्ख्यानां कर्मयोगेन योगिनाम् ॥ ३.३ ॥

loke'smin dvividhā niṣṭhā purā proktā mayānagha,
jñānayogena sāṁkhyānāṁ karmayogena yoginām. (3.03)

[Meaning] Śrī Krishna Said— In this world, O Arjuna, two types of *(niṣṭhā)* knowledge are in practice, as already told by me—theoretical knowledge as ordained in Sāṅkhya and practical knowledge as ordained in Yoga.

Thus, Jñāna implies theory, and Karma implies practical. So Sāṅkhya Darśana, as pointed out above, deals with the theory of embodiment and disembodiment of the soul, whereas the *Yogadarśana* deals with the practice of disembodiment of the soul. Lastly, I must say that Sāṅkhya Darśana is a key to understanding Vedānta, Upaniṣads, Vedas and other Śāstras. If one wants to understand Brahma Sūtras, Upaniṣad, he should meticulously go through Sāṅkhya.

In the present commentary, all concepts of Sāṅkhya have been explained easily so that the seekers of this excellent knowledge could benefit from the intended sense of the great author, Maharṣi Kapila. This is the first-ever translation that dives deep into the ocean of Sāṅkhya and shows the jewels to the gaze of all.

I must not forget to acknowledge the selfless help rendered by Alois Heinrich of Germany in bringing out this edition of Sāṅkhya.

Prof. Ravi Prakash Arya
Rohtak, Haryana

First Chapter

अथ त्रिविधदुःखात्यन्तनिवृत्तिरत्यन्तपुरुषार्थः ॥१॥

atha trividhaduḥkhātyantanivṛttiratyantapuruṣārthaḥ ǁ1 ǁ

(atha trividha-duḥkha atyanta nivṛttiḥ) Complete cessation of three types of pains (Ādhyātmika, Ādhidaivika and Ādhibhautika) is (atyanta-puruṣārthaḥ) the ultimate objective of human life.

Note: Ādhyātmika pain is caused by one's own kārmika sanskāras. Ādhidaivika pain is caused by natural calamities and Ādhibhautika pain is caused by material objects like sword, knife, stones etc.

न दृष्टात्तत्सिद्धिर्निवृत्तेरप्यनुवृत्तिदर्शनात् ॥ २ ॥

na dṛṣṭāttatsiddhirnivṛtterapyanuvṛttidarśanāt ǁ 2 ǁ

(tat siddhiḥ) Cessation of pain (na) cannot be achieved by (dṛṣṭāt) conventional means, (nvṛtteḥ api) because even after cessation of pain by conventional means (anuvṛtti-darśanāt) the recurrence takes place.

प्रात्याहिकक्षुत्प्रतीकारवत्तत्प्रतीकारचेष्टनात्पुरुषार्थत्वम् ॥ ३ ॥

prātyāhikakṣutpratīkāravattatpratīkāracheṣṭanātpuruṣārthatvam.

(pratīkāra cheṣṭanāt) Search for the means of cessation of pain is not going to help us (puruṣārthatvam) in achiving the goal of life [complete cessation of pain], as it recurs like (kṣut) hunger when (prātyāhika) daily (pratīkāra) obviated.

सर्वासंभवात्संभवेऽपि सत्त्वासंभवाद् हेयः प्रमाणकुशलैः ॥ ४ ॥

sarvāsambhavātsambhave'pi sattvāsambhavādheyaḥ
pramāṇakuśalaiḥ ǁ 4 ǁ

Through conventional means (sarva asambhavāt), it is not possible to eradicate pains completely. (sambhave api) Should we assume that complete eradication of pain is possible through conventional means? (sattā asambhavāt) Even then, the existence of pain cannot be eradicated, as the pain will continue to occur due to our new acts. Therefore, (heyaḥ) this mundane world pleasure should be abandoned by (pramāṇa kuśalaiḥ) the people who are experts in knowing [all these things through evidence].

उत्कर्षादपि मोक्षस्य सर्वोत्कर्षश्रुतेः ॥ 5 ॥

utkarṣādapi mokṣasya sarveātkarṣaśruteḥ ॥ *5* ॥

(mokṣasya utkarṣād api) Also, mokṣa is superior to all three other objectives of life (dharma, artha and kāma). (sarvotkarṣa) Vedic texts also confirm the superiority of mokṣa (śruteḥ).

For instance, Chhandogya Upaniṣad (8.12.1) says:

अशरीरं वासन्तं प्रियाप्रिये न स्पृशतः ।

aśarīram vā santam priyāpriye na spṛśataḥ ।

[Meaning] If a person is without body [in mokṣa], he cannot be touched by pain and pleasure.

Note: Here body means gross body [including buddhi, mind, sense organs and motor organs]

न हि वै सशरीरस्य सतः प्रियाप्रिययोरपहतिरस्ति ।

na hi vai saśarīrasya sataḥ priyāpriyayorapahatirasti ।

[Meaning] Should a person be in body, he cannot be immune to pain and pleasure.

अविशेषश्चोभयोः ॥ ६ ॥

aviśeṣaśchobhayoḥ ॥ *6* ॥

So far as the eradication of pain is concerned, (aviśeṣaḥ cha ubhayoḥ) there is no difference in both the means (conventional as well as Vedic means like yajña, dāna and tapa). Both means are not effective in the permanent eradication of suffering.

न स्वभावतो बद्धस्य मोक्षसाधनोपदेशविधिः ॥७॥

na svabhāvato baddhasya mokṣasādhaneāpadeśavidhi ॥ 7

By nature, the soul does not have a body, so the disembodiment of the embodied soul is taught in the Śāstras. (*svabhātaḥ baddhasya*) Had it been embodied by nature (*mokṣasādhana-upadeśa-vidhiḥ na*), there would have been no rule for its disembodiment (mokṣa).

If we consider the soul by nature embodied, then any instruction of mokṣa will be useless.

स्वभावस्यानपायित्वादननुष्ठानलक्षणमप्रामाण्यम् ॥ ८॥

svabhāvasyānapāyitvādananuṣṭhānalakṣaṇamaprāmāṇyam ॥8

Since (*svabhāvasya*) the essential nature is (*anapāyitvāt*) imperishable. If we consider that by nature, the soul is embodied or in bondage, the concept of mokṣa [disembodiment of soul] is not impossible. As such, (*anuṣṭhāna*) injunction of Śāstra (*na lakṣaṇa*) cannot be implemented. (*an-anuṣṭhāna lakṣaṇa*) Had the injunction of Śāstra not been implemented (aprāmāṇyam), it would not have held its authority.

नाशक्योपदेशविधिरुपदिष्टेऽप्यनुपदेशः ॥ ९ ॥

nāśakyopadeśavidhirupadiṣṭe'pyanupadeśaḥ ॥ 9 ॥

(Aśakya) Where there is (na śakya) impossibility of implementation of the rule, there is (na upadeśvidhiḥ) no rule made by Śāstra. Had the Śāstra (upadiṣṭeḥ) made a rule where execution is impossible (anupadeśaḥ), such a rule would have been treated as redundant or as if not ruled?

However, an objection is raised below regarding the perishability of the essential nature.

शुक्लपटवद्वीजवच्चेत् ॥ १० ॥

śuklapaṭavadbījavacchet ॥ 10 ॥

The rule of the imperishability of essential nature does not hold in the case of (śukla paṭ vat) white cloth [dyes destroy whiteness] and of seed [after germination, the original shape of seed changes].

Reply is given as under:

शक्त्युद्भवानुद्भवाभ्यां नाशक्योपदेशः ॥ ११ ॥

śaktyudbhavānudbhavābhyāṁ nāśakyopadeśaḥ ॥ 11 ॥

(Na) This example also does not support (upadeśaḥ) the injunction of rule (aśakyaḥ) where its execution is impossible. It merely talks about the appearance of the whiteness of cloth and the maintenance of the original shape of the seed on account of (śakti-anudbhava) absence of external force and change in whiteness and shape of the seed (śakti-udbhava) due to external force.

Objection: We may say that by nature, the soul remains disembodied but gets embodied by virtue of time. This objection is replied to below.

न कालयोगतो व्यापिनो नित्यस्य सर्वसंबन्धात् ॥ १२ ॥

na kālayogato vyāpino nityasya sarvasambandhāt ॥ 12 ॥

A soul (na) does not get embodied (kālayogataḥ) by virtue of time. Because time is (nityasya) eternal and (vyāpinaḥ) and all-pervasive, so (sarvasambandhāt) is related to the soul in all conditions (disembodiment or embodiment). That being so, a soul can never become disembodied.

Objection: We may say that the soul gets embodied by virtue of space. The reply is as follows:

न देशयोगतोऽप्यस्मात् ॥ १३ ॥

na deśayogato'pyasmāt ॥ 13 ॥

(na) Nor does the soul get embodied by virtue of space [from connection with space] (api) either (asmāt) for the same reason.

Objection: We may say that the soul gets embodied due to the condition. This objection is replied:

नावस्थातो देहधर्मत्वात्तस्याः ॥ १४ ॥

nāvasthāto dehadharmatvāttasyāḥ ॥ 14 ॥

(Na) Neither the soul gets embodied (avasthātaḥ) in consequence of condition because (tasyāḥ) the conditions, like birth, childhood, youth, old age and death, are (dehadharmatvāt) the property of the body and not the soul. Soul never passes through the conditions of birth, childhood, youth, old age and death.

असङ्गोऽयं पुरुष इति ॥ १५ ॥

asaṅgeā'yaṁ puruṣa iti ॥ 15 ॥

Because (ayaṁ puruṣaḥ) this soul is (asaṅgaḥ) is not associated with these conditions of the body. These conditions of the body do not affect the soul, the owner of the material body.

न कर्मणान्यधर्मत्वादतिप्रसक्तेश्च ॥ १६ ॥

na karmaṇānyadharmatvādatiprasakteścha ॥ 16 ॥

The soul is (na) not embodied (karmaṇi) as a

consequence of karmas [or kārmic sanskāras], (anyadharmatvāt) as the karmas [actions] are performed by mind, sense organs and body and not by the soul. The soul is not the performer of karmas [actions]. The soul is embodied (ati prasakteḥ cha) due to the extended association of karmas, done by mind, senses and body, to the soul.

Objection: If karmas are done by mind and body, then the mind should bear the fruits of karmas and not the soul. As such, the mind will be in bond with karma and not the soul. Then, the concept of mokṣa will be associated with the mind in bondage and not the soul, which is beyond the mind. The answer is given:

विचित्रभोगानुपपत्तिरन्यधर्मत्वे ॥ १७ ॥

vichitrabhogānupapattiranyadharmatve ॥ *17* ॥

Should mind and body be considered as the fruit bearer of karmas (anya-dharmatve) as the karmas are performed by them (vichitrabhogānupapattiḥ), the soul cannot have diverse experiences of pleasure and pain produced due to karmas. Therefore, although mind, senses and body perform karmas, their fruit is experienced by the soul.

So, we can say that the soul is not the doer of karmas but bhoktā [experincer] of the fruits of karmas.

Prakṛti [matter] alone cannot be the cause of the embodiment of the soul. The same is explained in the next sutra.

प्रकृतिनिबन्धनाच्चेन्न तस्या अपि पारतन्त्र्यम् ॥१८॥

Prakṛtinibandhanāchchhenna tasyā apim pāratantrayam ॥*18*॥

(Chet) If you say that (Prakṛti-nibandhanāt) embodiment of soul is caused by Prakṛti [body], (na) that is also not true because (tasyāḥ) Prakṛti [body] is (api) also (pāratantryam) dependant on other [soul]. Prakṛti [body] is controlled by chetana sattā [soul]. It cannot move an inch without being pushed by the soul.

From seventh sūtra onward till the present sūtra, the probable causes of an embodiment of the soul were discussed, and now the real cause of the embodiment of the soul is described.

ननित्यशुद्धबुद्धमुक्तस्वभावस्य तद्योगस्तद्योगादृते ॥ १९ ॥

na nityaśuddhabuddhamuktasvabhāvasya tadyogastadyogādṛte

॥ *19* ॥

The soul (svabhāvasya) which is by nature (nitya) eternal or free from birth and death, (śuddha) unchangeable, (buddha) conscious being, (mukta) not tainted by sattva, rajas and tamas guṇas of Prakṛti (na tadyogaḥ) so cannot be embodied or cannot get connected with the body (tadyogād ṛte) unless it comes in contact with Prakṛti [body].

Now the question arises as to why does soul come in contact with Prakṛti?

तद्योगोऽप्यविवेकान्नसमानत्वम् ॥ २० ॥

tadyogo'pyavivekānna samānatvam ॥ *20*॥

(tadyogaḥ) The contact of the soul with Prakṛti (avivekāt) is caused by aviveka [non-ability to distinguish itself from Prakṛti or non-ability to identify its true nature that I am pure spiritual element and not matter]. (asamāntvam) This cause is not similar to other causes responsible for the embodiment of the soul.

नियतकारणात्तदुच्छित्तिर्ध्वान्तवत् ॥ २१ ॥

niyatakāraṇāttaduchchhittirdhvāntavat ॥*21*॥

(tad ucchittiḥ) Removal of aviveka [non-ability to

distinguish soul from body and mind] is done by a (niyata-kāraṇāt) a fixed cause, i.e. viveka [ability to identify true nature of soul] as laid down in Sāṅkhya Śāstra, (dhvāntavat) like darkness is removed by the fixed cause, i.e. light.

प्रधानाविवेकादन्याविवेकस्य तद्धाने हानम् ॥२२॥

pradhānāvivekādanyāvivekasya taddhāne hānam ॥22॥

(pradhāna-avivekād) Aviveka [non-ability to distinguish between soul and Prakṛti, i.e. mind and body] gives rise to (anya-avivekasya) other aviveka like non-ability to understand that mind, body, sense organs, son, daughter, or wife, etc. do not form the part of our possession. (taddhāne) When the one aviveka [non-ability to distinguish between soul and Prakṛti] is removed, (hānam) the other aviveka [non-abiliy to understand that mind, body, sense organs, son, daughter or wife etc., do not form the part of our possession] is also removed.

वाङ्मात्रं न तुतत्त्वं चित्तस्थितेः ॥ २३ ॥

vāṅgmātram na tu tattvam chitta-sthiteḥ ॥ 23 ॥

(vāṅgamātram) Verbal information of distinction between soul and body [body here includes mind, intellect and sense organs also] (na tu tattvam) is not real, (chitta-sthiteḥ) because this information is stored in the mind.

When the soul identifies its true nature through samādhi, then only aviveka [non-ability to distinguish between soul and body] is removed, and mokṣa is attained.

युक्तितोऽपि न बाध्यते दिङ् मूढवदपरोक्षाद्दते ॥ २४ ॥

yuktito'pi na bādhyate diṅmūḍhavadaparokṣādṛte ॥ 24 ॥

This aviveka [ignorance to identify the soul with Prakṛti] is (na) not (bādhyate) removed (yuktitaḥ) even by arguments (api) and words, (dinmūḍhavat) like a person's illusion of direction cannot be removed by arguments and words (aparokṣād ṛte) until he realises himself.

Now, for the discrimination of Prakṛti and soul, we are bound to know all those entities that help us realise the soul. Many of them may not be perceived by our sense organs. For their perception, it is said:

अचाक्षुषाणामनुमानेन बोधो धूमादिभिरिववह्नेः ॥ २५ ॥

achākṣuṣāṇāmanumānena bodho dhūmādibhiriva vahe ॥ *25* ॥

(achākṣuṣāṇām) Imperceptible things (bodhah) are known by (anumānena) the means of inference, (iva) as (vahneḥ), and fire is known by (dhūmādibhiḥ) by smoke.

What are those imperceptible entities.

सत्त्वरजस्तमसां साम्यावस्था प्रकृतिः प्रकृतेर्महान्महतोऽहंकारोऽहंकारात्पञ्च तन्मात्राण्युभयमिन्द्रियं तन्मात्रेभ्यःस्थूलभूतानि पुरुष इति पञ्चविंशतिर्गणः ॥ २६

sattvarajastamasāṃ sāmyāvasthā Prakṛtiḥ prakṛtermahā-nmahato'haṃkāro'haṃkārātpañcha tanmātrāṇyubhayami-ndriyaṃ tanmātrebhyaḥ sthūlabhūtāni puruṣa iti pañchaviṃ-śatirgaṇaḥ ॥ *26* ॥

(sāmyāvasthā) The balanced state of (sattva-rajas-tamasāṃ) sattva [intelligence], rajas [motion] and tamas [inaction or inertia] (Prakṛtiḥ) is called Prakṛti [inactive energy]. (prakṛteh) From Prakṛti proceeds (mahān) cosmic intelligence containing exact information of the universal creation; (mahatah) from cosmic intelligence follows (ahaṅkārah) ahaṅkāra [individuatedness or discreteness]; (ahaṅkārāt) from ahaṅkāra proceeds (pañcha-tanmātrāṇi) five sensations [sound, touch, colour, taste and smell] and both external and internal sensations. External sensations are five sensory organs and five motor organs, and the internal sensation is the mind. (tanmātrebhyaḥ) From tanmātrās [sensations of perception] also follow (sthūlabhūtāni) their organs, e.g. from five sensations of perception [sound, touch, colour, taste and smell] follow particles constituting five states of matter called gross evolutes— ākāśa [space], vāyu [air or gases], agni [fire or heat and light], jala [waters or liquids] and pṛthivi [earth]. These, together with (puruṣa iti) the soul form the (gaṇaḥ) the group of (pañchaviṁśatiḥ) twenty-five.

Note: The above-cited whole process of creation represents the production of the soul's body in the mother's womb.

Here, one more thing must be noted that ahaṅkāra from the point of sattva, rajas and tamas guṇas is of three types— Taijas Ahaṅkāra, Vaikārika Ahaṅkāra and Bhūtādi Ahaṅkāra.

(1). From Taijas ahaṅkāra proceed mind, five sensory organs.

(2). From Vaikārika ahaṅkāra proceed motor organs.

(3). From Bhūtādi ahaṅkāra proceed five bhūta [matter/energy] tanmātras [sensations], and from five Bhūta [matter/energy] tanmātras proceed active matter particles [electrons, protons and neutrons] forming five gross elements [representing five states of matter].

How to know these.

स्थूलात्पञ्चतन्मात्रस्य ॥ २७ ॥

sthūlātpañchatanmātrasya ॥ *27*॥

(sthūlāt) From five states of matter, one can infer the existence of (pañcha-tanmātrasya) five tanmātras [sensations like sound, touch, colour, taste and smell].

बाह्याभ्यन्तराभ्यां तैश्चाहंकारस्य ॥ २८ ॥

bāhyābhyantarābhyāṁ taiśchāhaṁkārasya ॥ *28* ॥

(bāhyābhyantarābhyām) From external [five sensory organs and five motor organs], an internal sense [mind] and (taiḥ) tanmātrās [sensations of perception], we can infer the existence of ahaṅkāra [the factor of individuated-ness or discreteness or i-ness, my-ness].

तेनान्तःकरणस्य ॥ २९ ॥

tenāntaḥkaraṇasya ॥ *29* ॥

(tena) From ahaṅkāra (antaḥkaraṇasya) buddhi/mahat or intelligence is inferred.

ततः प्रकृतेः ॥ ३० ॥

tataḥ prakṛteḥ ॥ *30* ॥

(tataḥ) From mahat [intelligence], (prakṛteḥ) Prakṛti is inferred.

संहतपरार्थत्वात्पुरुषस्य ॥ ३१ ॥

saṁhataparārthatvātpuruṣasya ॥ *31* ॥

(puruṣasya) The existence of the soul is inferred (saṁhat-prārthatvāt) from the fact that these 24 products of Prakṛti are for someone else, i.e., for the soul and not for Prakṛti itself.

मूले मूलाभावादमूलं मूलम् ॥ ३२ ॥

mūle mūlābhāvādamūlaṁ mūlam ॥ *32* ॥

24 entities, except Puruṣa, have Prakṛti as their primitive material cause. (mule) Primitive material cause (mūlābhāvāt) has no other material cause, so (mūlam) primitive material cause is always (amūlam) causeless.

पारम्पर्येऽप्येकत्र परिनिष्ठेति संज्ञामात्रम् ॥ ३३ ॥

pāramparye'pyekatra pariniṣṭheti saṁjñāmātram ॥ *33* ॥

(paramparye api) Even if there is a succession of material causes (pariniṣṭhā), there must be (ektara) one endpoint of this succession. (it saṃjñāmatram) 'Prakṛti' is the name given to that endpoint, or we may say that endpoint is called 'Prakṛti'.

Now the question arises: what is the material cause of the creation or the bodies of living beings and the creation of the cosmos between the soul and Prakṛti? It is replied that:

समानः प्रकृतेर्द्वयोः ॥ ३४ ॥

samānaḥ prakṛterdvayoḥ ॥ 34 ॥

[Meaning 1] (dvayoḥ) Between two —soul and Prakṛti, (samānaḥ) it is proper to accept (prakṛteḥ) Prakṛti as the material cause of the bodies of souls or creation.

[Meaning 2] Prakṛti has two forms—sat and asat. In the form of sat, it is eternal, but in the form of asat, it continues to change. In its causal form, Prakṛti is sat, and in its product form, Prakṛti is asta. The sūtra says that (prakṛteḥ) Prakṛti is (samānam) the same irrespective of its (dvayoḥ) two forms.

In its sat form, the three guṇas are in a balanced state or remain inactive, but in its asat form, the three guṇas are imbalanced and become active. These three guṇas of Sāṅkhya are represented by three particles—electrons [sattva or -ve], protons [rajas or +ve] and neutrons [tamas or 0 charge]

Who is qualified for this knowledge?

अधिकारित्रैविध्यान्न नियमः ॥ ३५ ॥

adhikāritraividhyānna niyamaḥ ॥ 35 ॥

(adhikāri traividhyāt) Three types of persons are capable of receiving instructions—excellent, mediocre and inferior (na niyamaḥ), so not all need to arrive at the truth. Only the excellent are supposed to arrive at the truth.

महदाख्यमाद्यं कार्यं तन्मनः ॥ ३६ ॥

mahadākhyamādyaṁ kāryaṁ tanmanaḥ ॥ 36 ॥

(ādyaṁ kāryam) The first product of Prakṛti (mahadākhyam), called 'mahat', is nothing but the mind containing the information of the creation of bodies of living beings and cosmos.

चरमोऽहंकारः ॥ ३७ ॥

charamo 'haṁkāraḥ ॥ 37 ॥

(ahaṅkāraḥ) Ahaṅkāra [sense of individuality] is (charamaḥ) subsequent to it.

तत्कार्यत्वमुत्तरेषाम् ॥ ३८ ॥

tatkāryatvamuttareṣām ॥ 38 ॥

(uttareṣām) Others are (kāryatvam) product of (tat) that [ahaṅkāra].

आद्यहेतुता तद्द्वारा पारम्पर्येऽप्यणुवत् ॥ ३९ ॥

ādyahetutā taddvārā pāramparye'pyaṇuvat ॥ 39 ॥

(taddvārā pāramparye api aṇuvat) The tradition of dissolving succeeding macro effects [products] into their preceding micro causes, (aṇuvat) like atoms into their particles, also (ādyahetutā) establishes that Prakṛti is the indirect primitive cause of all its effects [products] in succession, starting from mahat to five macro evolutes (pañchabhūtas).

Since Prakṛti and soul are both eternal, why should we not accept that the dissolution of everything during decreation occurs in the chetana [sentient] soul rather than in jaḍa [insentient] Prakṛti? In this way, there will be no need to accept the existence of Prakṛti. The answer is given ahead:

पूर्वभावित्वे द्वयोरेकतरस्य हानेऽन्यतरयोगः ॥४०॥

pūrva bhāvitve dvayorekatarasya hāne'nyatarayogaḥ ॥

Since (dvayoḥ) both Prakṛti and soul are (pūrvabhāvitve) eternal and antecedent. (ekatarasya hāne) If the existence of one [Prakṛti] is denied (anyatarayogaḥ), the material causation will switch over to another [puruṣa]. But puruṣa does not qualify as the material cause, as puruṣa never undergoes change, and unchangeable things cannot be the material cause. The material cause must have the quality of change. Consequently, Prakṛti alone can be the material cause.

It is practically known that macro effects [products] dissolve into their micro causes. So, tanmātrās [sensations] may be considered the primitive material cause of this visible world. The answer is given below:

परिच्छिन्नं नसर्वोपादानम् ॥ ४१ ॥

parichchhinnaṁ na sarvopādānam ॥ 41 ॥

(parichchhinnam) What is limited (na) cannot be (sarvopādānam) the material cause of everything. Tanmātrās (sensations) are limited, so they cannot be the material cause of this whole material expanse. Prakṛti, being all-pervading, is the material cause of all things.

तदुत्पत्तिश्रुतेश्च ॥ ४२ ॥

tadutpattiśruteścha ॥ 42 ॥

(tadutpattiḥ) And the proposition that Prakṛti is the material cause of all is also proved (śruteḥ) from Vedic texts. For instance, the Ṛgveda (1.164.20) says:

द्वा सुपर्णा सयुजा सखाया समानं वृक्षं परिषस्वजाते ।

dvā suparṇā sayujā sakhāyā samānaṁ vṛkṣaṁ pariṣasvajāte I

[Meaning] Two birds [soul and universal soul] have taken shelter in a tree [Prakṛti].

Śvetāśvatara Upaniṣad (4.5) says:

अजामेकां लोहितशुक्लकृष्णां बह्वीः प्रजाः सृजमानां सरूपाः ।

ajāmekāṁ lohitaśuklakṛṣṇāṁ bahvīḥ prajāḥ sṛjamānāṁ sarūpāḥ

[Meaning] One eternal Prakṛti endowed with (lohita) rajas, (śukla) sattva and (kṛṣṇa) tamas guṇas (sṛjamānām) creates (bahvih prajāḥ) this whole material expanse (sarūpāḥ) which inherits its qualities.

When it is proved that Prakṛti is the only material cause of creation, again, there is a doubt that Prakṛti is not required; we may admit that creation takes place by accident. To this, the reply is as under:

नावस्तुनो वस्तुसिद्धिः ॥ ४३ ॥
nāvastuno vastusiddhiḥ ॥ 43 ॥

(vastusiddhiḥ) An entity (na) does not proceed (avastunaḥ) from non-entity.

If so, we may say that this world is non-entity. It originates by accident and will end by accident. In this regard, sūtrakāra says:

अबाधाददुष्टकारणजन्यत्वाच्च नावस्तुत्वम् ॥ ४४ ॥
abādhādaduṣṭakāraṇajanyatvāchcha nāvastutvam ॥ 44 ॥

(abādhāt) There is no hindrance in the existence of the world (cha) and (aduṣṭkāraṇa-janyatvāt) it is not the result of a faulty material cause, so (avastutvam) its being non-entity is (na) not proved.

Note: The continuity of the world's existence persists. During creation, it is in vyakta [visible form], and during decreation, it remains in (avyakta) invisible form in its primitive material cause.

This world is not the result of a faulty material cause. The Prakṛti is made of three guṇas, and these three guṇas are perceptible in created things or beings.

In support of the above argument, it is further observed:

भावे तद्योगेन तत्सिद्धिरभावे तदभावात्कुतस्तरांतत्सिद्धिः ॥ ४५ ॥

bhāve tadyogena tatsiddhirabhāve tadabhāvātkutastarāṁ

tatsiddhiḥ ॥ 45 ॥

(bhāve) In the presence of a primitive material cause (tatsiddhiḥ), the existence of its resultant world is established (tadyogena) by its connection with that primitive material cause. (abhāve) If the primitive material cause is absent (tad-abhāvāt), its resultant world will also be absent (kutastarām); in that case, (tatsiddhiḥ) how can the existence of the resultant world be proved?

As per Sāṅkhya Darśana, jaḍa [insentient] eternal Prakṛti is the material cause of creation, and chetana [sentient] Brahman is the efficient cause of creation. That means, Brahman is the Governor of Prakṛti and triggers it for creation. In such a condition, one can think that there is no need to admit the existence of Prakṛti as a material cause; the action [push] of Brahman may be considered as the material cause of the world.

न कर्मण उपादानायोगात् ॥ ४६ ॥

na karmaṇa upādānāyogāt ॥४६॥

(karmaṇaḥ) The action (na) cannot (upādānayogāt) be

associated with the material cause. So, Brahman's action creation does not prove Him to be the material cause of creation. He is the efficient cause.

Hence, it is essential to admit Prakṛti as the material cause of the world. After that, Prakṛti's utility for its help in attaining the goal of life (mokṣa) is established, as Prakṛti is responsible for the bhoga (enjoyment) and mokṣa of the soul. Prakṛti is the direct means of the bhoga (enjoyment) of the soul, for mokṣa also Prakṛti is indirectly responsible as mokṣa depends upon the ability of discrimination between Prakṛti and puruṣa. Had Prakṛti been absent, how would discrimination take place? Here, one may say that mokṣa can be attained by performing Śrauta karmas [directed in Vedas]; as there is no occasion for troubling ourselves about discrimination between the soul and the Prakṛti. To this, the reply is:

नानुश्रविकादपि तत्सिद्धिःसाध्यत्वेनावृत्तियोगादपुरुषार्थत्वम् ॥ ४७ ॥

nānuśravikādapi tatsiddhiḥ sādhyatvenāvṛttiyogā-
dapuruṣārthatvam ॥47॥

(tatsiddhiḥ na) Mokṣa cannot be achieved (ānuśravikāt api) by performing Śrauta karmas [yāgās]. Śrauta yāgas are performed to understand the process of creation. (sādhyatvena) These Śrauta karmas means of understanding the process of creation (āvṛttiyogāt), so these are repeated until the time the whole process of creation is comprehended. (apuruṣārthatvam) As such, they cannot be called a means to achieve the puruṣārtha [mokṣa].

Now the question arises: If they are not the means of puruṣārtha [the real goal of human life], what are the means of puruṣārtha?

तत्र प्राप्तविवेकस्यानावृत्तिश्रुतिः ॥ ४८ ॥

tatra prāptavivekasyānāvṛttiśrutiḥ ॥48॥

(prāptavivekasya) The discrimination (tatra) between the true natures of puruṣa and Prakṛti (anāvṛtti) leads to mokṣa (śrutiḥ), as per Vedic texts. For instance, according to the *Yajurveda* (31.18)

वेदाहमेतं पुरुषं महान्तमादित्यवर्णं तमसः परस्तात् ।

तमेव विदित्वाति मृत्युमेति नान्यः पन्थां विद्यतेऽयंनाय ॥

vedāhametaṁ puruṣaṁ mahāntamādityavarṇaṁ tamasaḥ parastāt /
tameva viditvāti mṛtyumeti nānyaḥ panthā vidyate'yanāya ॥

[Meaning] I have known this great and glorious soul endowed with the sun's brilliance as different from tamas (Prakṛti). Having realised this fact, man transcends the cycle of birth and death. There is no other way than this to the final freedom or mokṣa.

What is the fruit of the Śrauta karmas? It is explained hereunder:

दुःखादुःखं जलाभिषेकवन्न जाड्यविमोकः ॥ ४९ ॥

duḥkhādduḥkhaṁ jalābhiṣekavanna jāḍyavimokaḥ ॥ 49॥

Śrauta karmas involve various types of pain. So (duḥkhāt) karmas involving multiple kinds of pains (duḥkham) will cause pain ultimately, (jāḍyavimokaḥ na) they cannot remove aviveka [non-discrimination between the soul and Prakṛti], (vat) as there is no (jāḍya vimokaḥ) relief from pain caused by cold by (jalābhiṣeka) taking bath into waters.

काम्येऽकाम्येऽपिसाध्यत्वाविशेषात् ॥ ५० ॥

kāmye'kāmye'pi sādhyatvāviśeṣāt ॥ 50॥

(kāmye) The kāmya karmas [actions done with some

desire] are (sādhyatvāt) helpful in fulfilling desires and not attaining mokṣa, similarly (akāmye) akāmya karmas [actions done without any selfish motive] (sādhyatvāt) are helpful in purification of mind and not attaining mokṣa, so (aviśeṣāt), so they are not directly helpful in attaining mokṣa.

We can say that the fruits of kāmya and akāmya karmas help achieve the temporary goals of life but not the permanent goal of life called puruṣārtha.

निजमुक्तस्य बन्धध्वंसमात्रं परं न समानत्वम् ॥५१॥

nijamuktasya bandhadhvaṁsamātrṁ paraṁ na
samānatvam ॥51॥

(bandhadhvaṁsa-mātram) Disembodiment [freedom from the bondage of Prakṛti] is (param) the ultimate goal of (nija-muktasya) the soul willing its liberation. Therefore, (samānatvam na) there is no parity between viveka-jñāna [discrimination between soul and Prakṛti] and fruits of kāmya or akāmya karmas.

The existence of jaḍa [insentient] Prakṛti, and chetana [sentient] soul has been established above, but all these entities are examined by pramāṇa [means of knowledge]. So, hereunder the nature of pramāṇa is discussed.

द्वयोरेकतरस्य वाप्यसंनिकृष्टार्थपरिच्छित्तिः प्रमा । तत्साधकतमं यत्तत् त्रिविधं प्रमाणम् ॥ ५२ ॥

dvayeārekatarasya vāpyasaṁnikṛṣṭārthaparichchhittiḥ pramā ।
tatsādhakatamaṁ yattat trividhaṁ pramāṇam ॥ 52॥

(pramā) Right knowledge means (asaṁnikṛṣṭārtha-parichchhittiḥ) the determination of something that has previously been unknown. This type of determination can be done (dvayoḥ) by both—the buddhi under the guidance of the soul (api vā) or (ekatarasya) buddhi alone [in view of its past experience]. (tatsādhakatamam) The means of pramā [right knowledge] is called called pramāṇa. (yat tat trividhaṁ pramāṇam) That prāmāṇa [means of knowledge] is of three types—Śabda [Vedic texts or the words of a seer or high profile yogī], anumāna [inference] and pratyakṣa [sensory perception]. These three means of knowledge have been described above.

Now, the question is whether these three means of knowledge are sufficient or if more means of knowledge are required. The reply is:

तत्सिद्धौ सर्वसिद्धेर्नाधिक्यसिद्धिः ॥ ५३ ॥

tatsiddhau sarvasiddher nādhikyasiddhiḥ ॥ 53 ॥

(tat siddhau) If these three means of knowledge are established (sarvasiddheḥ), everything can be ascertained (ādhikya siddhiḥ na), and no more means of knowledge are required to be established.

Having already given the general definition of pramāṇa [means of knowledge], next, the definition of various means of knowledge [pramāṇas] is given.

यत्संबद्धंसत्तदाकारोल्लेखि विज्ञानं तत् प्रत्यक्षम् ॥ ५४ ॥

yatsambaddhaṁ sattadākārollekhi vijñānaṁ tatpratyakṣam ॥ 54

(pratyakṣam) Pratyakṣa [perception] is (tat) that (vijñānam) knowledge (yet) which results (sat sambaddham) from the right connection of sense organs with the external objects and (tadākārollekhi) portrays their exact form.

Someone may say that this definition of pratyakṣa is faulty, as it does not extend to the pratyakṣa of the yogīs, who can perceive past and future things. To this, the reply is given as follows:

योगिनामबाह्यप्रत्यक्षत्वान्न दोषः ॥ ५५ ॥

yogināma-bāhya-pratyakṣatvānna doṣaḥ ॥ 55 ॥

(na doṣaḥ) There is no fault in this definition (yoginām abāhya-pratyaṣatvāt) because the perception of yogīs is not an external one. The perception of yogīs is an internal one. So, here, the term pratyakṣa [perception] stands for both external and internal pratyakṣa [perception].

लीनवस्तुलब्धातिशयसंबन्धाद्वाऽदोषः ॥ ५६ ॥

līna vastu labdhātiśayasaṁbandhādvādoṣaḥ ॥ 56 ॥

(vā adoṣaḥ) Or there is no fault in this definition because yogīs, through the great power of yoga, are able (labdhātiśaya-sambandha) to establish close connections with (līna vastu) things hidden in their material cause or intervened by time, distance and another object. We may call it yogic pratyakṣa.

ईश्वरासिद्धेः ॥ ५७ ॥

īśvarāsiddheḥ ॥ 57 ॥

[First Meaning] The above definition is not faulty. Had the Yogic pratyakṣa not been included in the definition of pratyakṣa, (Īśvara-asiddheḥ) existence of Īśvara would not have been proved by pratyakṣa pramāṇā. Yogic pratyakṣa rules out the non-existence of Īśvara since the yogīs can have a perception of Īsvara through samādhi.

Here, a seeker can raise doubt about why we should not accept Īśvara as the material cause of the creation and discard the existence of prakṛti as the material cause. To this, the reply can be given through the second meaning of the sūtra.

[Second Meaning] (Īśvara-asiddheḥ) Īśvara cannot be established as the material cause of the world. He is the efficient cause of the world. For example, potter is the efficient cause of the pot, whereas clay is the material cause of the pot. Like the potter, Īśvara is the efficient cause; like clay, prakṛti is the material cause of creation.

From the above sūtra, it is crystal clear that Sāṅkhya admits the existence of Īśvara but does not admit Him to be the material cause of the world.

How can he be not proved as the material cause of the creation?

मुक्तबद्धयोरन्यतराभावान्न तत्सिद्धिः ॥ ५८ ॥

muktabaddhayoranyatarābhāvānna tatsiddhiḥ ॥ *58*॥

[First meaning] (na tat siddhiḥ) Proof of Īśvara as the material cause of the world cannot be established because he is (anyatarābhāt) different from (muktabaddhayoḥ) both liberated and bonded.

He is neither liberated nor bonded. Had he been liberated or bonded, we could have said that decreation is caused under His liberation and creation is caused under His bondage. However, in the case of His being liberated, He would not undergo the change required for creation; in the case of His being bonded, He cannot attain the status of Īśvara being connected with dharma or adharma.

उभयथाप्यसत्करत्वम् ॥ ५९ ॥

ubhayathāpyasatkaratvam ॥ *59*॥

(ubhayathā ap) Should we take Īśvara both for liberated or bonded, even then He cannot be proved as a material cause. In both the conditions [liberated and bonded], he will be a chetana sattā [sentient entity] and (asatkaratvam) chetana [sentient] cannot convert/transform or manifest itself into achetana [insentient], as this material creation is achetana [insentient].

Now the question arises when Īśvara is not proven to be the material cause of this material creation, then why are the Śrutis eulogising Īśvara as the cause of creation? The answer is as follows:

मुक्तात्मनः प्रशंसाउपासासिद्धस्य वा ॥ ६० ॥

muktātmanah praśaṁsā upāsā siddhasya vā ॥ 60 ॥

(praśaṁsā) Śrutis [Vedic texts] are doing eulogy (muktātmanah) either of liberated souls (vā) or of (upāsā-siddhasya) Īśvara who is attainable through upāsanā (meditation), so their statements should not be taken as the proof of Īśvara as the material cause of this world.

Now the question arises: if Īśvara is not the material cause of the world, what is His role as creator? The answer is:

तत्संनिधानादधिष्ठातृत्वं मणिवत् ॥ ६१ ॥

tatsaṁnidhānādadhiṣṭhātṛtvaṁ maṇivat ॥ 61 ॥

(saṁnidhānāt) On account of proximity (tat) to Prakṛti, (adhiṣṭhātṛtvaṁ) Īśvara plays the role of governor or superintendence [efficient cause of creation]. Insenient Prakṛti cannot move by itself without being forced by some sentient power. Due to the proximity of Īśvara, Prakṛti receives motion and transforms into this visible material expanse. This may be compared with (maṇivat) magnet and iron. Just as a magnet's proximity generates a motion in iron, similarly, due to the proximity of Īśvara, a motion is generated in Prakṛti.

Note: Inactive energy [Prakṛti] is called dark energy or tamas. Due to the proximity of Īśvara, dark energy [inactive energy] is activated.

From the foregoing discussion, it is proved that Prakṛti plays the role of the material cause of the world. As such, all past or future effects [products] will merge with Prakṛti as their primary cause. A yogī, through his power of yoga, can establish contact with Prakṛti and perceive the past and future.

After describing the Governorship or Superintendentship of Īśvara, the governorship or superintendentship of souls with respect to individual actions of their bodies is also explained in the ensuing sūtra [succint aphorism].

विशेषकार्येष्वपि जीवानाम् ॥ ६२ ॥

viśeṣakāryeṣvapi jīvānām ॥ 62 ॥

Governorship or Superintendentship (jīvānām) of souls is (api) also seen in (viśeṣa-kāryeṣu) the individual movements or actions of bodies, such as seeing, hearing, thinking, etc. Various tendencies or movements in the bodies are possible only on account of the proximity of the soul.

Now the question arises: if the soul is the governor of the individual actions of its body, it should have the knowledge to govern because only a knowledgeable person can be a governor. The answer is that the soul has the cognitive power to gain knowledge. The proof of the cognitive power of the soul is given in the following sūtra.

सिद्धरूपबोद्धृत्वाद्वाक्यार्थोपदेशः ॥ ६३ ॥

siddharūpaboddhṛtvādvākyārtheaupadeśaḥ ॥ 63 ॥

(siddharūpa-boddhṛtvāt) Since the soul has cognitive power, (vākyārthopadeśaḥ) instructions have been given for it in the Śāstras.

Note: Instructions of the Śāstras and Vedas are meant to enhance the knowledge of the soul. Had the soul not had cognitive power, instructions in the Śāstras and Vedas would not have been needed.

It is often seen that knowledge is the subject matter of buddhi, so why should we not say that buddhi has both cognitive and governorship power rather than the soul?

अन्तःकरणस्य तदुज्ज्वलितत्वाल्लोहवदधिष्ठातृत्वम् ॥ ६४ ॥

antaḥkaraṇasya tadujjvalitatvāllohavadadhiṣṭhātṛtvam ॥ 64 ॥

(antaḥkaraṇasya) Buddhi seems (adhiṣṭhātṛtvam) to have cognitive power or governorship (tad ujjavalitatvāt) because it is enlightened by the soul (lohavad) as is the case of iron. As the iron is made red-hot by fire, just so the buddhi is enlightened by the soul.

Buddhi, in itself, has no cognitive power or governorship; rather, the soul's reflection on it gives it the cognitive power or power of governorship. Hence, the soul actually has both the cognitive and governing powers, not buddhi [intellect].

The discussion on pratyakṣa pramāṇa [means of knowledge] has ended. In that context, it was also established that Īśvara [God] is not the material cause of creation but rather an efficient cause. Now, the definition of anumāna pramāṇa [inference as a means of knowledge] is given.

प्रतिबन्धदृशः प्रतिबद्धज्ञानमनुमानम् ॥ ६५ ॥

pratibandhadṛśaḥ pratibaddhajñānamanumānam ॥ 65 ॥

(pratibaddhajñānam) Knowledge of connection through the perception of connection on the part of (pratibandh-dṛśaḥ) a person who knows the permanent connection between them is called inference. For instance, there is the permanent connection of smoke with fire [and not of fire with smoke]. A person who knows this connection. He may identify the connected [fire] through the perception of its connection with [smoke].

Now definition of Śabda pramāṇa [statement as means of knowledge] is given.

आप्तोपदेशः शब्दः ॥ ६६ ॥

āptopadeśaḥ śabdaḥ ॥ *66* ॥

(āptopadeśaḥ) A statement of a high profile seer [or yogī] who has obtained the exact knowledge of things realisation in samādhi (śabdaḥ) stands in the category of Śabda pramāṇa.

Note: Exact and perfect knowledge received in samādhi through realisation is called āpti. Āpta are those who have āpti.

The purpose of pramāṇas [means of knowledge], is explained hereunder:

उभयसिद्धिः प्रमाणात्तदुपदेशः ॥ ६७ ॥

ubhayasiddhiḥ pramāṇāttadupadeśaḥ ॥ *67* ॥

(pramāṇāt) Using pramāṇas [means of knowledge], the existence of both—chetana [sentient-soul and Brahman] and achetana [insentient-Prakṛti] is established (tad upadeśaḥ); hence, there is instruction about them.

After defining various pramāṇas, now the question arises with what pramāṇa, existence of both chetana [sentient] and achetana [insentient] is established?

सामान्यतोदृष्टादुभयसिद्धिः ॥ ६८ ॥

sāmānyato dṛṣṭādubhayasiddhiḥ ॥ *68* ॥

(ubhayasiddhiḥ) The Existence of both sentient and insentient entities is established (sāmānyatodṛṣṭāt) by sāmānyatodṛṣṭa anumāna pramāṇa [inference of invisible entity based upon universal experience].

Note: Inference is of three types.

1. Pūrvavat [inference of product or effect from cause]: In this inference, we infer the unperceived effect from a seen cause. For example, we can predict the coming rain by seeing dark, thick clouds.

2. Śeṣavat [inference of cause from effect or product]: An inference in which the unobserved cause is inferred from the seen effect [product]. For example, a quick muddy water movement in the river can be used to infer past rain.

3. Sāmānyatodṛṣṭa [inference of invisible entity based upon universal experience]: The inference is drawn from the universal experience and is applied to cognise invisible objects or things based on the same experience. For example, universal experience tells us that any effect [product] owes its origin to the cause of the same class, such as golden ornaments originating in gold.

Similarly, we find three guṇas operating in all objects of the world, so we can infer some invisible material cause consisting of three guṇas called Prakṛti.

We find that houses, beds, motorcars, etc., are various means not made to serve the purpose of some material thing but to serve the purpose of some sentient entity [chetana sattā]. All material things that undergo change have the same character. So, a universal rule is inferred that all material objects undergoing change are made to serve a sentient entity. Thus, from sāmānyatodṛṣṭa inference, the existence of an invisible sentient entity is established.

Now the question arises as to who is the actual beneficiary of the knowledge gained through prāmāṇas (means of knowledge)— Buddhi or Soul? The answer is given below:

चिदवसानो भोगः ॥ ६९ ॥

chidavasāno bhogaḥ ॥ 69 ॥

Bhoga means experiencing pain and pleasure as a result of karmas. (bhogaḥ) The Experience of pain and pleasure (chid-avasānaḥ) ends with the soul. So, whatever knowledge is gained through pramāṇās, the soul is the end beneficiary. Buddhi is material, so it acts as an instrument. Only a sentient entity can be the beneficiary.

Karmas are done by buddhi, mana and body, but the result of karmas done by the body is experienced [bhoga] by the soul. This material world is for the benefit of the soul. The maker of the material world is Īśvara [Supreme being], but the soul takes its benefit. How is it? The answer is given through a customary example:

अकर्तुरपि फलोपभोगोऽन्नाद्यवत् ॥ ७० ॥

akarturapi phalopabhogo'nnādyavat ॥ 70 ॥

(akartuḥ api) Sometimes, a non-doer (phalopabhogaḥ) may also enjoy the fruit of action (annādyavat), like food. The mother cooks the food, but others also enjoy it in the family. So, the soul enjoys the fruit of work done by the body.

Now the real solution is given.

अविवेकाद्वा तत्सिद्धेः कर्तुः फलावगमः ॥ ७१ ॥

avivekādvā tatsiddheḥ kartuḥ phalāvagamaḥ ॥ 71 ॥

(tat siddheḥ) Having proved the fact that the non-doer soul enjoys the result of work done by the body (avivekād vā), there is a wrong notion due to aviveka [ignorance] (phalāvagamaḥ) that the result belongs to (kartuḥ) body, the actual doer of the action.

Is there any condition where the soul gets rid of aviveka

and bhoga [experience of pain and pleasure]? The answer is given below:

नोभयं च तत्त्वाख्याने ॥ ७२ ॥

nobhayaṁ cha tattvākhyāne ॥72॥

(tattvākhyāne) When the truth is revealed that the soul is not a physical/material body [or when the soul identifies its true nature] (na ubhayam), the soul gets rid of both—aviveka [non-ability to identify its true nature] and bhoga [experience of pain and pleasure about karmas done by the body].

Having discussed the means of knowledge [pramāṇas], the existence of soul and Prakṛti is established. Now, the hurdles on the way of pratyakṣa pramāṇa will be discussed.

विषयोऽविषयोऽप्यतिदूरादेर्हानोपादानाभ्यामिन्द्रियस्य ॥ ७३ ॥

viṣayo'viṣayo'pyatidūrāderhānopādānābhyāmindriyasya ॥ 73 ॥

(viṣayaḥ) An object of sense organs (aviṣayaḥ ap) may not qualify to be an object (atidūrāgeḥ) in consequence of great distance and closest proximity due to (indriyasya hānāt) failure of sense organs and (upādānāt) intervention by another object.

Prakṛti is also the object of sense-organs. Is there any hurdle to its not being the object of sense-organs?

सौक्ष्म्यात्तदनुपलब्धिः ॥ ७४ ॥

saukṣamyāttadanupalabdhiḥ ॥ 74॥

(saukṣmyāt) Because of subtlety (tad anupalabdhiḥ), the Prakṛti is not perceptible.

How can we establish its existence if it is not perceptible because of its subtle form? The reply is:

कार्यदर्शनात्तदुपलब्धेः ॥ ७५ ॥

kāryadarśanāttadupalabdheḥ ॥ 75 ॥

(tadupalabdheḥ) The existence of subtle Prakṛti is established (kāryadarśanāt) by beholding its effects [product].

वादिविप्रतिपत्तेस्तदसिद्धिरिति चेत् ॥ ७६ ॥

vādivipratipattestadasiddhiriti chet ॥ 76 ॥

Moreover, (chet) if (tad-asiddhiḥ) the existence of Prakṛti is not established, (vādivipratipatteḥ) because of the contradictory arguments of other disputants, then you will find an answer in the following aphorism.

तथाप्येकतरदृष्ट्यैकतरसिद्धेर्नापलापः ॥ ७७ ॥

tathāpyekataradṛṣṭyaikatara siddhernāpalāpaḥ ॥ 77 ॥

Whatever the arguments. All have admitted the principle of cause and effect. (tathāpi) As such (ekatara dṛṣṭyā) beholding of the product [effect] (ekatara-siddheḥ), the existence of cause (na apalāpaḥ) cannot be denied.

How is it that Prakṛti alone is the primitive material cause and no other entity? To this, the reply is:

त्रिविधविरोधापत्तेः ॥ ७८ ॥

trividhavirodhāpatteḥ ॥ 78 ॥

If we were to infer any other cause other than Prakṛti (trividha-virodhāpatteḥ), we would find the [other cause] contradicting the three guṇās seen in the world. Hence, Prakṛti, consisting of three guṇas, is only the ideal primitive material cause of the world.

Whether the products already exist before they arise, this doubt is repealed in the following sūtra.

नासदुत्पादो नृश्रृङ्गवत् ॥ ७९ ॥

nāsadutpādo nṛśṛṅgavat ॥ 79॥

(asadutpātaḥ) Production of non-entity (na) is not possible, (nṛśṛṅgavat) such as man's horn.

The above aphorism propounds the most coveted doctrine of 'Satkāryavāda' [kārya or effect always exists in its cause]. Further arguments are given to establish this doctrine [that effect already exists in its cause before its origin].

उपादाननियमात् ॥ ८० ॥

upādānaniyamāt ॥ 80॥

(upādāna-niyamāt) Because there is a rule that there must be some material cause for every product [effect].

Why is there an essentiality of material cause for an effect [product]? The answer is given below.

सर्वत्र सर्वदा सर्वासंभवात् ॥ ८१ ॥

sarvatra sarvadā sarvāsambhavāt ॥ 81॥

(sarva-asambhavāt) Because everything is not produced (sarvatra) everywhere and (sarvadā) and always.

Had there been no essentiality of material cause, everything could have been produced everywhere. But this is not possible.

शक्तस्य शक्यकरणात् ॥ ८२ ॥

śaktasya śakyakaraṇāt ॥ 82॥

(śaktasya śakyakārṇāt) A material cause can produce the effect [product] according to its potential.

A material cause can produce a specific effect [product] and not every effect [product] as per its potentiality. This proves that effect [product] exists in its material cause even before its production.

This again proves the existence of effect [product] even before its production. Like in a seed: the potential flower already exists in the seed before it is grown.

कारणभावाच्च ॥ ८३ ॥

kāraṇabhāvāchcha ॥ *83* ॥

(kāraṇa-bhāvāt cha) Due to the prior existence of effect [product] in its cause, production of non-entity is not possible. Only an entity can be produced.

Now the question arises: if effect [product] already exists in its material cause, why do we discuss its production? Sūtrakāra raises the same doubt.

न भावे भावयोगश्चेत् ॥ ८४ ॥

na bhāve bhāvayogaśchet ॥84॥

(chet) If we say (bhāve) that the effect [product] already exists in its material cause, (na) it is not correct to (bhāva-yogaḥ) associate the effect [product] with production.

If an effect [product] already exists in its material cause, then we should not discuss its production.

The doubt is resolved in the next sūtra.

नाभिव्यक्तिनिबन्धनौ व्यवहाराव्यवहारौ ॥ ८५ ॥

nābhivyaktinibandhanau vyavahārāvyavahārau ॥85॥

(na) It is incorrect to say that we should not discuss the production of effect [product] if it already exists in its material cause. (vyavahāra-avyavahārau) The employment or non-employment of the term 'production' or 'existence' (abhivyakti-nibandhanau) is occasioned by the manifestation and non-manifestation of the effect [product].

The effect [product] exists in its material cause in unmanifest form. So long as it remains unmanifested, we use the term 'existence'. We use the term 'production' as soon as it is manifested. Moreover, the effect becomes functional upon its manifestation, not its non-manifestation. If the effect remains functional even in its unmanifest form, then in the decreation [unmanifest] phase also, the world can function and creation [manifestation] is not required.

The effect [product] exists even before its production/manifestation. After the phase of manifestation [production], it again undergoes the phase of unmanifestation, known as the destruction of effect [product]. The author defines the 'destruction'.

नाशः कारणलयः ॥ ८६ ॥

nāśaḥ kāraṇalayaḥ ॥86॥

(kāraṇalayaḥ) Merging of effect [product] into its cause is called 'destruction' of effect [product]. But this destruction does not mean 'non-existence'.

पारम्पर्यतोऽन्वेषणा बीजाङ्कुरवत् ॥ ८७ ॥

pāramparyato'nveṣaṇā bījāṅkuravat ॥87॥

(pāramparyaḥ) The continuum of manifestation and unmanifestation should be (anveṣaṇā) understood (bījāṅkuravat) by the example of the continuum of seed and sprout.

Just as there is an unending tradition of seed producing a sprout and sprout producing a seed, similarly, the manifestation ends [results] into unmanifestation, and unmanifestation ends [results] into manifestation.

उत्पत्तिवद्वाऽदोषः ॥ ८८ ॥

utpattivadvā'doṣaḥ ॥88॥

Manifestation and production connote the same thing. (adoṣaḥ) There is no problem with the term manifestation (utpatti-vad), such as 'production'.

Just as the produced effect [product] cannot be reproduced, similarly manifested effect [product] cannot be remanifested. The only difference is that in the use of the term 'production', it appears as if the effect [product] was non-existent before its production, and in the use of the term 'manifestation', it appears as if the effect [product] existed even before its manifestation. This difference has already been addressed through various arguments.

The cause can be inferred from the effect [product]. Now, the properties of the effect [product] are described.

हेतुमदनित्यं सक्रियमनेकमाश्रितं लिङ्गम् ॥ ८९ ॥

hetumadanityaṁ sakriyamanekamāśritaṁ liṅgam ॥91

(hetumat) The effect [product] is that which has a material cause, (anityaṁ) which is perishable, (sakriyam) which has motion [atoms moving in it], (anekam) which has multiple forms, (āśritam) which is dependant upon its material cause, (liṅgam) which ultimately merges into its material cause.

Thus, all effects [product] in their causal form are similar to the cause, but their effectual [production] form differs from their cause. The above properties of effect [product] also establish the dissimilarity between cause and effect. This similarity and dissimilarity between effect and cause is further established in the next sūtra.

आञ्जस्यादभेदतो वा गुणसामान्यादेस्तत्सिद्धिःप्रधानव्यपदेशाद्वा ॥ ९० ॥

āñjasyādabhedato vā guṇasāmānyādestatsiddhiḥ
pradhānavyapadeśādvā ॥90॥

(āñjasyāt) From direct perception [pratyakṣa], the dissimilarity between cause and effect is established, e.g. direct perception of clay [cause] and pot [effect] establishes dissimilarity between the two. (vā) Or (abhedataḥ) from similarities (guṇasāmānyādeḥ) of general qualities of effects [for example, holding water is the general quality similar to all effects, i.e. pots] the difference between effects [pots] and their cause [clay] is established, e.g. pots can hold water, but clay cannot hold it. (vā) Or (tat siddhiḥ) the difference between effect and cause is also established (vyapadeśāt) by śabda pramāṇa, for instance, (pradhāna vyapadeśa) Prakṛti [material cause of world] finds a separate mention in Vedas and other Śāstras than its effect [the world].

Thus, the similarity and dissimilarity between cause and effect is accepted by Sāṅkhya. In the causal state, the effect is similar to its cause, but in the effectual state, the effect is dissimilar to its cause.

The properties common to material cause and its effect [product] are described in the next sūtra.

त्रिगुणाचेतनत्वादि द्वयोः ॥ ९१ ॥

triguṇāchetanatvādi dvayoḥ ॥91॥

(dvayoḥ) Both material cause and effect are (triguṇāchetanatvādi) made of three guṇas [sattva, rajas and tamas], and both are non-sentient [jaḍa].

After describing the common properties of material cause and effect. The next sūtra describes dissimilar properties of three guṇas [sattva, rajas and tamas].

प्रीत्यप्रीतिविषादादैगुणानामन्योन्यं वैधर्म्यम् ॥ ९२ ॥

prītyaprītiviṣādādyairguṇānāmanyonyaṁ vaidharmyam ॥92

(guṇānām) Three guṇas [sattva, rajas and tamas] are (vaidharmyam) different (anyonyam) from each other because of their different properties. Sattva guṇa is endowed with the fundamental property of prīti [attraction], rajas has aprīti [repulsion] as its fundamental property, and tamas has viṣāda [neutrality] as its fundamental property.

Note: These three guṇas — sattva, rajas and tamas are operative in three material particles called electrons, protons, and neutrons. In living beings' sattva guṇa is reflected in their attractive or pleasing personality, rajoguṇa is reflected in their displeasing personality, and tamoguṇa is reflected in dejectedness.

Due to the above-cited fundamental properties of sattva, rajas and tamas guṇas, particles also have the tendency of attraction-repulsion [electrons and protons] and neutrality [neutrons].

लघ्वादिधर्मैरन्योन्यं साधर्म्यं वैधर्म्यं गुणानाम् ॥ ९३ ॥

laghvādidharmairanyonyaṁ sādharmyaṁ vaidharmyaṁ
guṇānām ॥93 ॥

The present sūtra deals with two contexts

[Meaning in the context of the property of Guṇas of Prakṛti]

(laghvādidharmaiḥ) Through their respective properties of lightness, motion and gurutva [mass] (guṇānām), three guṇas —sattva, rajas, and tamas have (sādharmyam) similarity among themselves and (vaidharmyam) dissimilarity (anonym) from each other. For instance, the property of lightness is similar to all sattvaguṇas but different from rajas and tamas guṇas. Similarly, the property of motion is similar to all rajas guṇas but different from sattva and tamas guṇas, and so forth. Maharṣi Kapila has clarified that Prakṛti is not an individual entity but is constituted of sattva, rajas and tamas; these constituents are numerous. Had there been only one sattva, rajas and tamas, the question of similarity would not have arisen.

[Meaning in the context of the property of particles of Prakṛti or matter]

The second meaning of the above sūtra reflects the properties of matter particles. It says that matter particles have three main properties inherited from three guṇas of Prakṛti, as they are the product of these three guṇas. They are formed from Bhūtādi [tamas] ahaṅkāra in combination with Taijas [sāttvika] and Vaikārika [rājasika ahaṅkāra]. The property of sattva guṇa is lightness, the property of rajoguṇa is motion, and the property of tamoguṇa is gurutva [mass]. So the matter particles—electrons, protons and neutrons have a property of lightness, as they are extremely small and light; particles of matter are constantly moving, as they have the property of motion; and each particle has mass, as they have the property of gurutva. In the context of the properties of matter particles, the meaning is as under:

(laghvādidharmaiḥ) Through the properties of lightness, motion and gurutva [heaviness] (guṇānām), of three matter particles —taijas [electrons], vaikārika [protons] rajas and bhūtādi [neutrons] have (sādharmyam) similarity among themselves and (vaidharmyam) dissimilarity from each other. For instance, the property of lightness makes all particles similar, but the same also cause differences between them. For example, taijas particles [electrons] are the lightest of all, vaikārika [protons] are heavier than electrons but lighter than bhūtādi particles [neutrons]. Similarly, the property of gurutva [mass] is similar to all particles, but bhūtādi particles have comparatively more mass than the other two, and so more inertia. The property of motion is similar to all particles, as they are constantly moving. Still, they differ from each other because of the difference in motion in several ways—for example, electrons have a -ve charge; protons have +ve, whereas neutrons have no charge; because of this difference in charge, they have a difference of motion. Maharṣi Kapila has clarified that Prakṛti is not an individual entity but is constituted of sattva, rajas and tamas guṇās at the invisible level, which is reflected in electrons, protons and neutrons at the visible level. These constituents are numerous. Had there been only one sattva, rajas and tamas, or one electron, proton and neutron, the question of similarity would not have arisen

Now it is established that mahat [buddhi or intelligence] and rest are effects [products].

उभयान्यत्वात्कार्यत्वं महदादेर्घटादिवत् ॥ ९४ ॥

ubhayānyatvātkāryaṁtvaṁ mahadāderghaṭādivat ॥94॥

(ubhayānyatvāt) Being different from both — Puruṣa and Prakṛti, that are void of material cause, (mahadādeḥ) intelligence and the rest are the effects [products] as pots and the like.

Mahat [buddhi] in the cosmos is cosmic sāntelligence as far as cosmic creation is concerned; in the individual, it is individual intelligence as far as the individual soul's embodiment called birth is concerned.

परिणामात् ॥ ९५ ॥

pariṇāmāt ||95||

(pariṇāmāt) Because of their ever-changing nature, intelligence and rest are effects [products] of Prakṛti.

समन्वयात् ॥ ९६ ॥

samanvayāt ||96||

They are products (samanvayāt) because of their coherence with their inherent cause [material cause] Prakṛti.

Because they are perfectly connected with their material cause, and the qualities of material cause are seen in them. The same is supported from different angles.

शक्तितश्चेति ॥ ९७ ॥

śaktitaścheti ||97||

(iti cha) And, finally, it can be argued that mahat [intelligence] and others are effects (śaktitaḥ) because they are qualified instruments or resources for the bhoga (enjoyment) of the soul.

Mahat and others are effect, it is proved by reverse argument in the next sūtra.

तद्धाने प्रकृतिः पुरुषो वा ॥ ९८ ॥

taddāne Prakṛtiḥ puruṣo vā ||98||

(tad hāne) If mahat and others are not considered effects (Prakṛti puruṣo vā) they will sit in the category of Prakṛti or puruṣa because only these two elements do not come in the category of effects.

If one argues that mahat and others may be assigned a different category from both non-effects, Prakṛti and puruṣa, the reply is given in the next sūtra.

तयोरन्यत्वे तुच्छत्वम् ॥ ९९ ॥

tayoranyatve tuchchhatvam ॥99॥

(anyatve) If they [mahat and others] are considered distinct from (tayoḥ) both Prakṛti and puruṣa (tuchchhatvam), then we shall have to accept them as non-existent because the existence of any material element is impossible without Prakṛti.

कार्यात्कारणानुमानं तत्साहित्यात् ॥ १०० ॥

kāryātkāraṇānumānaṁ tatsāhityāt ॥100॥

(kāraṇānumanam) Cause is inferred (kāryāt) from the effect, (tatsāhityāt) because the effect merges into its cause.

Note: The tradition of merging of effects into their causes is technically known as 'kāryasāhitya'.

अव्यक्तं त्रिगुणाल्लिङ्गात् ॥ १०१ ॥

avyaktaṁ triguṇāllingāt ॥101॥

(avyaktam) Prakṛti is inferred from (lingāt) its mergent [effect] mahat (triguṇāt) attributed with three guṇas-sattva, rajas and tamas.

तत्कार्यतस्तत्सिद्धेर्नापलापः ॥ १०२ ॥

Tatkāryatastat siddhernāpalāpaḥ ॥102॥

(tatsiddheḥ) Since the existence of Prakṛti follows (tatkāryataḥ) from its effects. Like mahat and others, the existence of Prakṛti (na) cannot be (apalāpaḥ) denied.

The existence of Prakṛti is established because of its effects [products]. But the existence of the soul cannot be established for want of its effects [products]. The reply to this objection is given in the next sūtra.

सामान्येन विवादाभावाद्धर्मवन्न साधनम् ॥ १०३ ॥

sāmānyena vivādābhāvāddharmavanna sādhanam ॥103॥

(sāmānyena) Generally, (abhāvāt) there is no (vivād) dispute regarding the existence of the soul [everybody accepts the existence of the soul] (dharmavat) like that of dharma [all accept the essentiality of dharma], so for the understanding of the existence of the soul, (na) no particular (sādhanam) means is required.

However, the actual position of the soul is explained in the next sūtras.

शरीरादिव्यतिरिक्तः पुमान् ॥ १०४ ॥

śarīrādivyatiriktaḥ pumān ॥104॥

(pumān) The soul is (vyatiriktaḥ) distinct (śarīrāt) from body. Body is not soul.

संहतपरार्थत्वात् ॥ १०५ ॥

saṁhataparārthatvāt ॥105॥

It is seen that (saṁhāt) conglomeration of material things is always (parārthatvāt) for the use of some other [chetana] entity.

This body [conglomeration of five gross evolutes] is for the use of the soul. Through the body, the soul performs its activities.

त्रिगुणादिविपर्ययात् ॥ १०६ ॥

triguṇādiviparyayāt ॥106॥

The soul is (viparyāt) opposite to (triguṇādi) three guṇās called sattva-rajas and tamas forming the matter [body].

अधिष्ठानान्चेति ॥ १०७ ॥

adhiṣṭhānāchcheti ॥106॥

The soul is (adhiṣṭhānāt cha iti) the superintendent of this body. [Similarly, Brahman is the superintendent of this material universe].

भोक्तृभावात् ॥ १०८ ॥

bhoktṛbhāvāt ॥108॥

The soul is (bhoktṛbhāvāt) bhoktā (enjoyer or experiencer) of this material world.

The material world is meant for bhoga (experience or enjoyment) of the soul. This material world is made of five gross evolutes of Prakṛti [pṛthivī, jala, agni, vāyu, ākāśa], and the Human body, the highly advanced body system, has five sense organs or five receptors. Through these receptors, the soul of human beings does the bhoga or enjoys the creation made of five gross evolutes.

कैवल्यार्थं प्रवृत्तेः ॥ १०९ ॥

kaivalyārtham pravṛtteḥ ॥109॥

The soul has the (pravṛtteḥ) tendency towards (kaivalyārtham) kaivalya [mokṣa or separation from material body].

We see human beings striving for happiness. All desires end up in a vicious circle. Everybody has a dislike for losing, and losing creates a passion for winning, so ultimately, happiness brings pain. So we have to erase future pains. This brings us to real happiness [kaivalya].

जडप्रकाशायोगात्प्रकाशः ॥ ११० ॥

jaḍaprakāśāyogātprakāśaḥ ॥110॥

(jaḍa) Material things (ayogāt) cannot be transformed into (prakāśa) chetana [immaterial] souls, so existence of the soul (prakāśaḥ) is itself proved.

निर्गुणत्वान्न चिद्धर्मा ॥ १११ ॥

nirguṇatvānna chiddharmā ‖111‖

Since the soul is (nirguṇatvāt) devoid of sattva-rajas and tamas guṇas, it cannot fit in the category of dharma [guṇa] and dharmī [guṇī or holder of guṇas]. Soul is chidasvarūpa [chetana or sentient itself], (chiddharmā na) chetanā [sentientness] is not the quality of the soul.

श्रुत्या सिद्धस्य नापलापस्तत्प्रत्यक्षबाधात् ॥ ११२ ॥

śrutyā siddhasya nāpalāpastatpratyakṣabādhāt ‖112‖

(siddhasya) What is established (śrutyā) by Vedic texts (na aplāpaḥ) cannot be denied, although the (pratyakṣa-bādhāt) common perception does not hold the soul to be devoid of guṇas.

सुषुप्त्याद्यसाक्षित्वम् ॥ ११३ ॥

suṣuppatyādyasākṣitvam ‖113‖

Had the soul not been pure chetanā [sentientness], it would not have been a witness at suṣupti [deep sleep], svapna [dream] and jāgrat [awake] states.

जन्मादिव्यवस्थातः पुरुषबहुत्वम् ॥ ११४ ॥

janmādivyavasthātaḥ puruṣabahutvam ‖114‖

(puruṣabahutvaṁ) The multiplicity of souls follows (janmādivyasthātaḥ) from the system of different births.

Different souls take different births according to different sanskāras. These different births prove the existence of multiple souls.

According to some scholars, one soul pervades various bodies. Due to the diversity of bodies, souls appear diverse. Their argument in support of their contention is as follows:

उपाधिभेदेऽप्येकस्य नानायोग आकाशस्येव घटादिभिः ॥ ११५ ॥

upādhibhede'pyekasya nānāyoga ākāśasyeva ghaṭādibhiḥ ॥115

(upādhi-bhede) Given the diversity of upādhis [various bodies], (ekasya) one soul (nānāyoga) has diverse bodies as its adjuncts, (iva) just as (ākāśasya) one space has (ghaṭādibhiḥ) various pots as its adjuncts.

उपाधिर्भिद्यते नतु तद्वान् ॥ ११६ ॥

upādhirbhidyate natu tadvān ॥116 ॥

(upādhiḥ) Bodies (bhidyate) are different, (natu) not (tadvān) their owner [the soul].

The reply to the above argument is given as follows:

एवमेकत्वेन परिवर्तमानस्य न विरुद्धधर्माध्यासः ॥ ११७ ॥

Evamekatvena parivartamānasya na viruddhadharmīdhyāsaḥ ॥
117

(evam) If (ekatvena) one soul (pari-vartamānasya) pervades uniformly all diverse bodies, it (na) cannot (adhyāsaḥ) feel (viruddha-dharma) contradictory attributes.

अन्यधर्मत्वेऽपि नारोपात्तत्सिद्धिरेकत्वात् ॥ ११८ ॥

anyadharmatve'pi nāropāttatsiddhirekatvāt ॥118 ॥

(api) Should we consider (anyadharmatve) the attributes of pain, pleasure, bondage, mokṣa etc., as belonging to the mind and (āropāt) implant them into the soul, then also, we (na tat siddhiḥ) cannot achieve the aim of proving the existence of only one soul pervading all bodies uniformly, as (ekatvāt) one soul simultaneously cannot be in bondage and mokṣa.

However, the Vedic texts speak of one soul, so the principle of multiple souls would contradict the statements of

Vedic texts.

नाद्वैतश्रुतिविरोधो जातिपरत्वात् ॥ ११९ ॥

nādvaitaśrutivirodho jātiparatvāt ॥119॥

The principle of diversity of soul is not going to (advaita-śruti-virodhaḥ) contradict the Vedic statements that propound advaita [oneness of the soul], as here the term advaita (oneness) stands for (jāti paratvāt) genus [nature] and not an entity. That means there is advaita [oneness] in the nature of souls. It does not stand for one soul. In other words, there are many souls, but all souls are one so far as their nature [like imperishability, chetanatā or sentientness etc.] is concerned.

Who can know sentient [chetana] nature of all souls? The answer is given in the next sūtra.

विदितबन्धकारणस्य दृष्ट्या तद्रूपम् ॥ १२० ॥

viditabandhakāraṇasya dṛṣṭyā tadrūpam ॥120॥

(tadrūpam) This sentient nature of souls is known (dṛṣṭyā) only by the eyes of a yogī who has (vidit) known the (bandha-kāraṇasya) cause of bondage through samādhi and has identified the true nature of his soul [viveka].

Common persons do not have this type of experience, so how do we accept the authenticity of your argument? The author replies-

नान्धादृष्ट्या चक्षुष्मतामनुपलम्भः ॥ १२१ ॥

nāndhādṛṣṭyā chakṣuṣmatāmanupalambhaḥ ॥121॥

(na andh-adṛṣṭyā) If things are not seen by the blind, that does not mean that (chakṣumatām) people with eyesight (anupalambhaḥ) can not perceive them.

In other words, what is unknown to a common person

does not follow that the same will not be known to a learned person.

वामदेवादिर्मुक्तो नाद्वैतम् ॥ १२२ ॥

vāmadevādirmukto nādvaitam ॥122॥

History tells that Vāmadeva and others have been liberated, which shows that there is no advaita [one soul]. If only one soul existed, one person's liberation would have entailed the liberation of all living persons.

NB: These arguments are not against Vedānta Darśana, but the neo-Vedāntists. The Vedānta Darśana does support the idea of one soul, but it is the postulation of neo-Vedāntists.

The question is, should we accept multiple souls, some in bondage and some in mokṣa? There will be a time when all the souls will attain mokṣa, and this world will be deserted. The answer is given in the forthcoming sūtra.

अनादावद्य यावदभावाद्द्विष्यदप्येवम् ॥ १२३ ॥

anādāvadya yāvadabhāvādbhaviṣyadapyevam ॥123॥

(abhāvāt) This has not happened [world has not deserted due to all souls' attaining mokṣa] (anādau adya yāvat) from the beginningless time to date, and (abhaviṣyat) there is no possibility (evam) of it in future.

इदानीमिव सर्वत्र नात्यन्तोच्छेदः ॥ १२४ ॥

idānīmiva sarvatra nātyantochchhedaḥ ॥124॥

(iva) Just as (idānīm) today, (na atyantochchhedaḥ), we do not see the absolute abolition of souls; the same did not happen and will not occur at any time.

The question is, would this world continue in the same state? Answer is-

व्यावृत्तोभयरूपः ॥ १२५ ॥

vyāvṛttobhayarūpaḥ ॥125॥

This world is (vyavṛttaḥ) excluded (ubhaya-rūpaḥ) from both states.

The first state is that there will be absolute eradication forever at some time. The second state is that this world will continue forever as it is. Both these states are not going to happen. Neither will this world be eradicated forever, nor will it continue forever as it is.

After establishing the multiplicity of souls, various other characteristics of souls are described. Just as Brahman is the Superintendent of Prakṛti, the soul is the superintendent of the body, and it is the witness [indirectly experiencer] of all experiences. Here, one may ask a question: if witnessing is the nature of the soul, it will continue to enjoy the nature of witness, so it cannot attain mokṣa. The author replies:

साक्षात्संबन्धात्साक्षित्वम् ॥ १२६ ॥

ṣākṣātsaṁbandhātsākṣitvam ॥126॥

To be a witness is not the primary nature of the soul. (sākṣāt saṁbandhāt) Due to its connection with the body, (sākṣitvam) it is a witness.

What is the primary nature of the soul?

नित्यमुक्तत्वम् ॥ १२७ ॥

nityamuktatvam ॥127॥

Eternal liberation from Prakṛti is the primary nature of the soul.

औदासीन्यं चेति ॥ १२८ ॥

audāsīnyaṁ cheti ॥128॥

(cha) And (iti) finally, the nature of the soul is (audāsīnyaṁ) indifference to doership. The soul is not a doer. But the doership of the soul is mentioned in the Śāstras. How is this to be justified? To this, the author replies:

उपरागात्कर्तृत्वं चित्सान्निध्याच्चित्सान्निध्यात् ॥ १२९ ॥

uparāgātkartṛtvaṁ chitsānnidhyāchchitsānnidhyāt ‖129 ‖

(kartṛtvam) The soul's thinking of being a doer (uparāgāt) results from the influence of (chit) mind replete with information from the outside world, which is (sānnidhyāt) close to it [soul].

Second Chapter

In the first Chapter, the subject matter of the Sāṅkhya Darśana was described. The existence of Prakṛti and Puruṣa [soul] and their various characteristics have been explained. In the second chapter, the process of embodiment of the soul and the body's production from Prakṛti will be described in detail. At the outset, the purpose of the creation is explained.

विमुक्तमोक्षार्थं स्वार्थं वा प्रधानस्य ॥ १ ॥

vimuktamokṣārtham svārtham vā pradhānasya ॥ 1 ॥

Creation takes place (mokṣārtham) for the liberation of the soul (vimukta), which is basically liberated, and for (pradhānasya) Prakṛti presenting (svārtham) itself for the bhoga (enjoyment) of the soul.

If creation is aimed at mokṣa, all souls should be liberated after creation. Thus, the creation in future will become redundant. To this, replies the author-

विरक्तस्य तत्सिद्धेः ॥ २ ॥

viraktasya tatsiddheḥ ॥ 2 ॥

Mokṣa does not take place through the creation once and for all, but (tatsiddhiḥ) it is attained through (viraktasya) renunciation achieved after excessive pains of many deaths, births and sicknesses.

न श्रवणमात्रात्तत्सिद्धिरनादिवासनाया बलवत्त्वात् ॥ ३ ॥

na śravaṇamātrāttatsiddhiranādivāsanāyā balavattvāt ॥ 3 ॥

This vairāgya [renunciation] is (na tatsiddhiḥ) not attained (śravaṇamātrāt) by the mere hearing the preachings or reading of scriptures on renunciation because the soul has accumulated (balavattvāt) powerful mundane world (vāsanāyāḥ) sanskāras (anādi) from time immemorial.

The author gives one more argument to support the continuous flow of creation.

बहुभृत्यवद्वा प्रत्येकम् ॥ ४ ॥

bahubhṛtyavaddā pratyekam ॥ 4 ॥

(bahubhṛtyavad-vā) Just as a person who has many persons dependent on him continues his efforts (pratyekam) till each one of them is supported, this creation has endless souls dependent on it for its support. The flow of this creation continues endlessly until all souls attain mokṣa.

Here, one may have a doubt that all activities of Prakṛti leading to the manifestation of creation are superintended by Brahman, as it is said in Taittirīya Saṁhitā:

एतस्मादात्मनः आकाशः सम्भूतः ।

etasmādātmanaḥ ākāśaḥ sambhūtaḥ.

[Meaning] Due to Brahman's agitation of the Prakṛti [inactive energy], this Bhūtākāśa [illuminated with active energy] originated.

If this Prakṛti can do nothing without being activated by Brahman, in this case, we should say that Prakṛti's existence is unreal and bhoga and mokṣa are attained by souls due to the inspiration of Brahman. To this, replies the author—

प्रकृतिवास्तवे च पुरुषस्याध्याससिद्धिः ॥ ५ ॥

Prakṛtivāstave cha puruṣasyādhyāsasiddhiḥ ॥ 5 ॥

(Prakṛti-vāstave) Because Prakṛti's existence is real (puruṣasya adhyāsa-siddhiḥ), that is why does the soul falsely assume itself to be Prakṛti [manifested into the body].

NB: Adhyāsa is a false assumption of the material body in

the soul and the soul in the material body.

Now, one may ask who is responsible for bhoga and mokṣa of the soul- Prakṛti or its effect [body]? To this replies the author-

कार्यतस्तत्सिद्धेः ॥ ६ ॥

kāryatastatsiddheḥ ॥ *6* ॥

(kāryataḥ tatsiddhiḥ) The effect of Prakṛti [body] is responsible for bhoga and mokṣa of the souls.

Without a body, a soul can't achieve bhoga or mokṣa.

If the body is responsible for the bhoga and mokṣa of a soul, why do all the souls not attain bhoga and mokṣa equally? The answer is given in the next sūtra-

चेतनोद्देशान्नियमः कण्टकमोक्षवत् ॥ ७ ॥

chetanoddeśānniyamaḥ kaṇṭakamokṣavat ॥ *7* ॥

(niyamaḥ) Attainment of bhoga and mokṣa (uddeśāt) depends upon the condition of (chetana) the soul. (kaṇṭaka-mokṣavat) Just as an aware person can escape from a thorn, an ignorant person may be trapped; similarly, an enlightened person can safely escape the trap of the mundane world, but an ignorant gets trapped in it.

Here, one may suggest that the statement of sūtra no. 5 that the soul falsely assumes itself as the body is incorrect. Here, it can be maintained that the soul transforms into buddhi (intellect), mind, etc. in conjunction with Prakṛti. To this, replies the author-

अन्ययोगेऽपि तत्सिद्दिर्नाञ्जस्येनायोदाहवत् ॥ ८ ॥

anyayoge'pi tatsiddirnānañjasyenāyodāhavat ॥ *8* ॥

(api) Even though (anya-yoge) there be the conjunction

of the soul with the other [body], (tatsiddhiḥ) the power of manifestation (na) does not exist in the soul (āñjasyena) directly. Instead, it is Prakṛti that manifests. (ayo-dāha-vat) Just as the red-hot iron is not going to burn. Instead, the fire conjunct with iron causes burns.

It has already been stated that the objective of creation is bhoga and mokṣa of the soul. Now, the process of embodiment of the soul is stated.

रागविरागयोर्योगः सृष्टिः ॥ ९ ॥

rāgavirāgayoryogaḥ sṛṣṭiḥ ॥ 9 ॥

[Meaning in the case of creation of soul's body] The soul's body is created by the conjunction of rāga (ovum) and virāga (sperm). Ovum is āgneya [-ve] and sperm is somīya [+ve].

[Meaning in the creation of the material universe] The above sūtra also applies in the case of the creation of the material universe. Accordingly, its meaning will be as follows: (sṛṣṭiḥ) This material creation takes place by (yogaḥ) a combination of atoms caused as a consequence of (rāga) attraction and (virāga) and repulsion of atoms.

In the original state of Prakṛti, sattva, rajas, and tamas guṇas are also balanced, so they cannot create anything. When this balance is disturbed, they attract and repulse, and combinations form, resulting into creation.

In view of the same, it is said-

अग्निसोमात्मकमिदं सर्वम् ।

agni-ṣomātmakam idam sarvam.

Everything is made up of the āgneya (-ve) and somīya (+ve) elements.

महदादिक्रमेण पञ्चभूतानाम् ॥ १० ॥

mahadādikrameṇa pañchabhūtānām ॥ 10 ॥

When sperm (male gamete) fuses with ovum (female gametes), (pañchabhūtānām) a body made of five bhūtas [evolutes of Prakṛti] is formed (mahadādi-krameṇa) in order of mahat (intelligence) and others.

A zygote is formed with the fusion of sperm and ovum when the suitable soul takes entry into the sperm at the time of fusion. The first one to evolve in the zygote is intelligence, followed by ahaṅkāra [discreteness] applied to the mind, sensations of perception, sensory organs, and five sensations of actions and their motor organs. This sequence has already been explained in Sāṅkhya.

आत्मार्थत्वात्सृष्टेनैषामात्मार्थ आरम्भः ॥ ११ ॥

ātmārthatvātsṛṣṭenaiṣāmātmārtha ārambhaḥ ॥ 11 ॥

(sṛṣṭeḥ) The formation of the body constituted of the mahat [intelligence] and others is (ātmārtham) for the sake of the soul [to serve the soul's interest]. (eṣām) They (na) do not form the body (ātmārtha) for their own sake.

Since the objective of the body is to provide the soul with the facility of bhoga and mokṣa, which can possibly be experienced by the soul. Mahat and others are made of matter, so the concepts of bhoga and mokṣa cannot apply to them.

Here, a question arises: in the sequence of creation of mahat, etc., from Prakṛti, dik [directions] and kāla [time] have been missed, although they form the essential part of the creation of the world. To this, replies the author-

दिक्कालावाकाशादिभ्यः ॥ १२ ॥

dikkālā vākāśādibhyaḥ ॥ *12* ॥

(dik-kālau) Dik [directions] and kāla [calculable time] are formed from (ākāsādibhyaḥ) ākāsa [bhūtākāsa or elemental space] of the cosmos [not from the ākāsa of the body]. Here, in the Sāṅkhya Darśana, five bhūtas [evolutes] do not belong to the cosmos but to the body. So, dik and kāla have not been enumerated. They will be enumerated when the creation of five external evolues [pṛthivī, jala, agni, vāyu and ākāsa] will be discussed.

Now, the nature and functions of mahat [intelligence] and others in the body are explained in order.

अध्यवसायो बुद्धिः ॥ १३ ॥

adhyavasāyo buddhiḥ ॥ *13* ॥

(buddhiḥ) The nature of mahat [buddhi] is (adhyavasāyaḥ) to ascertain the information gathered by the mind.

तत्कार्यं धर्मादिः ॥ १४ ॥

tatkāryaṁ dharmādiḥ ॥ *14* ॥

(tatkāryam) Function of mahat [buddhi] is (dharmādiḥ) to know the intended meaning of the Śāstras and Vedas. Mimānsā Darśana says:

चोदना लक्षणोऽर्थो धर्मः ।

Chodanā lakṣaṇo'artho dharmaḥ.

[Meaning] Dharma is a figurative meaning of the Veda.

NB: Buddhi can know the intended sense of Śāstras and Vedas when it is dominated by sattvaguṇa. What happens when it is dominated by rajoguṇa or tamoguṇa? The answer is given in the next sūtra.

महदुपरागाद्विपरीतम् ॥ १५ ॥

mahaduparāgāddiparītam ॥ *15* ॥

When (mahat) Buddhi is dominated by (uparāgāt) tamas and rajoguṇa, (viparītam) it becomes reversed. It cannot understand the intended sense of Vedas and Śāstras. It is full of adharma, ignorance, and attachment and becomes devoid of spiritual powers.

Now the nature of ahaṅkāra is defined.

अभिमानोऽहंकारः ॥ १६ ॥

abhimāno'haṁkāraḥ ॥ *16* ॥

(ahaṅkārah) Ahaṅkāra is (abhimānah) the sense of individuality [I and my].

एकादशपञ्चतन्मात्रं तत्कार्यम् ॥ १७ ॥

ēkādaśapañchatanmātraṁ tatkāryam ॥ *17* ॥

Eleven senses [mind, five sense organs and five motor organs] and five tanmātrās [sensations of perception, like sound, touch, sight, taste and smell] are the effects [products] of Ahaṅkāra.

There are three types of ahaṅkāra—sāttvika, rājasika and tāmasika. Now the question arises: which type of ahaṅkara produces which kind of effect or product?

सात्विकमेकादशकं प्रवर्तते वैकृतादहंकारात् ॥१८॥

sātvikamekādaśakaṁ pravartate vaikṛtādahaṁkārāt ॥*18*॥

(sāttvikam ekādaśakam) Sāttvika group of 11 senses [five senses of perception, five senses of action and mind] (pravartate) proceed (vaikṛtāt) from vaikṛta [sāttvika] (ahaṅkārat) ahaṅkāra.

What is that sāttvika group of 11 senses? Explains author himself as under:

कर्मेन्द्रियबुद्धीन्द्रियैरान्तरमेकादशकम् ॥ १९ ॥

karmendriyabuddhīndriyairāntaramekādaśakam ॥ *19* ॥

Mind, the internal sense is eleventh if counted, along with five external motor senses and five senses of perception.

अहङ्कारिकत्वश्रुतेर्न भौतिकानि ॥ २० ॥

ahaṅkārikatvaśruterna bhautikāni ॥ *20* ॥

(ahaṅkārikatva śruteḥ) Since this sāttvika group of 11 senses is the product of ahaṅkāra, they are (na) not (bhautikāni) physical organs.

One may raise a doubt that in the Bṛhadāraṇyaka Upaniṣad (3.2.13), the sense organs like vāk, prāṇa and chakṣu are described as being absorbed into devatās like Agni, Vāyu and Āditya respectively. For example,

अग्निं वागप्येति वातं प्राणश्चक्षुरादित्यम् ।

agniṁ vāgapyeti vātaṁ prāṇaśchakṣurādityam.

[Meaning] Vāk is absorbed in Agni, prāṇa in Vāyu and Chakṣu in Āditya.

As per the law of nature, a product or effect gets absorbed into its cause. The above statement of Bṛhadāraṇyaka Upaniṣad shows that vāk[speech] is a product of agni devatā, prāṇa [breathing] is a product of vāyu devatā and chakṣu [eye] is the product of āditya (sun) devatā. As such, the opinion of the author that sense organs are the product of Ahaṅkāra is not tenable. The answer to this is given below:

देवतालयश्रुतिनारम्भकस्य ॥ २१ ॥

devatālayaśrutinārambhakasya ॥ *21* ॥

(devatā-laya śruti) Wherever in Upaniṣads senses are referred to as being absorbed by Agni and other devatās (anārambhakasya), those references do not refer to absorption by their cause just as the absorption of water into the earth does not mean that the earth is the cause of water.

Some thinks that Mind is eternal, the author replies:

तदुत्पत्तिश्रुतेर्विनाशदर्शनाच्च ॥ २२ ॥

tadutpattiśrutervināśadarśanāchcha ॥ 22 ॥

Mind is not eternal (tadutpatti-śruteḥ) as its origin is talked about in Śāstras and (vināśa-darśanāt cha) its decay is seen in old age.

Other characteristics of senses are also described by the author-

अतीन्द्रियमिन्द्रियं भ्रान्तानामधिष्ठाने ॥ २३ ॥

atīndriyamindriyaṁ bhrāntānāmadhiṣṭhāne ॥ 23 ॥

(indriyam) Senses are (atīndriyam) supersensuous [beyond the reach of other senses]. (adhiṣṭhāne) To identify senses with their sense organs is a (bhrāntānām) mistaken notion.

In Sāṅkhya, there are 11 senses. One may argue that one should accept one single sense, which, through the diversity of powers, performs diverse actions. The author refutes this argument-

शक्तिभेदेऽपि भेदसिद्धौ नैकत्वम् ॥ २४ ॥

śaktibhede'pi bhedasiddhau naikatvam ॥ 24 ॥

(bheda-siddhau) If the difference is established even (śakti-bhede) by the difference of powers, (naikatvam) singleness of sense is not proved.

Further the diversity of senses is supported.

न कल्पनाविरोधः प्रमाणदृष्टस्य ॥ २५ ॥

na kalpanāvirodhaḥ pramāṇadṛṣṭasya ॥ 25 ॥

(pramāṇa-dṛṣṭasya) What has been known by proofs (na) cannot be (kalpanā-virodhaḥ) set aside by conjectures.

Eleven senses are established based on their reception, functions, and the anatomy of the body.

उभयात्मकं मनः ॥ २६ ॥

ubhayātmakaṁ manaḥ ॥ 26 ॥

Mind is associated with both senses of perception [sense-organs] and senses of action [motor-organs].

गुणपरिणामभेदान्नानात्वमवस्थावत् ॥ २७ ॥

guṇapariṇāmabhedānnānātvamavasthāvat ॥ 27 ॥

(guṇa-pariṇāma-bhedāt) Due to the variety of sense organs , one single mind produces various perceptions when it associates with them, like the conditions of childhood, youth, and old age belonging to one single person.

NB: The mind is the internal sense of perception, and the five sense organs are located in the body externally. One single internal sense [mind], in association with five external receptors, makes various perceptions; for example, when it is associated with the eyes produces colour sensation, with ear hearing sensation, with nose smell sensation, and so on.

रूपादिरसमलान्त उभयोः ॥ २८ ॥

rūpādirasamalānta ubhayoḥ ॥ 28 ॥

(ubhayoḥ) The objects of both senses of perception and senses of action (rūpādi-malānta) begin with colour and end with excretion.

The five sense organs and their objects are: eyes for

colour, ears for sound, nose for smell, tongue for taste, and skin for touch.

The five senses of action and their functions are: mouth for speaking, legs for walking, hands for grasping, (pāyu) genitals for procreation and (upastha) anus for excretion.

द्रष्टृत्वादिरात्मनः करणत्वमिन्द्रियाणाम् ॥ २९ ॥

draṣṭṛtvādirātmanaḥ karaṇatvamindriyāṇām ॥ 29 ॥

(ātmanaḥ) The soul is (draṣṭṛtvādi) the preceptor, (indriyāṇām) senses organs are (karaṇatvam) mere instruments.

NB: The senses are receptors, but the receiver is the soul. The soul cannot receive anything without these receptors. Similarly, actions are done by the five organs of actions, but the inspiration comes from the soul.

Now, the author mentions the unique functions of all three internal senses: Buddhi, Ahaṅkāra and Manas.

त्रयाणां स्वालक्षण्यम् ॥ ३० ॥

trayāṇāṁ svātlakṣaṇyam ॥ 30 ॥

The three - Buddhi, Ahaṅkāra and Manas possess their unique characteristics.

Buddhi's unique function is to ascertain the information gathered by the mind and intended sense of Śāstras and Vedas.

The notion of individuality is the unique function of Ahaṅkāra.

Gathering information [saṅkalpa] and emptying information [vikalpa] is the unique function of the mind called [chitta].

सामान्यकरणवृत्तिः प्राणाद्या वायवः पञ्च ॥ ३१ ॥

sāmānyakaraṇavṛttiḥ prāṇādyā vāyavaḥ pañcha ॥ 31 ॥

Five prāṇas [vital airs]— prāṇa, udāna, vyāna, samāna and apāna— are the combined function of all three internal senses [Buddhi, Ahaṅkāra, Mind].

All three internal senses are combinedly called the mind.

क्रमशोऽक्रमशश्चेन्द्रियवृत्तिः ॥ ३२ ॥

kramaśo'kramaśaśchendriyavṛttih ॥ 32 ॥

(indriyavṛttiḥ) The functions of the senses may take place (kramaśaḥ) in an ordered way (cha) and (akramaśaḥ) in a disordered way.

An example of ordered function— Having seen a thief by faint light, the perceiver first determines the thief's presence with his eyes. He gathers this information in his mind and associates his presence to himself with the help of ahaṅkāra that he is coming towards him and will take away his money. Finally, buddhi decides that he should either leave this place or catch him.

An example of Simultaneous function — Seeing a tiger, a person runs away instantly. In this case, the functions of the four organs take place simultaneously, e.g., when the eyes see the tiger, the mind gathers the information about the presence of the tiger, ahaṅkāra associates the presence of the tiger to himself that the tiger may attack him, and buddhi decides to run away. In this case, functions of senses have taken place in successive order, but this succession of functions is so instant that it appears to be happening simultaneously.

वृत्तयः पञ्चतय्यः क्लिष्टाक्लिष्टाः ॥ ३३ ॥

vṛttayaḥ pañchatayyaḥ kliṣṭākliṣṭāḥ ॥ 33 ॥

When the mind is exposed to objects of the external world, five vṛttis (states) develop. They may be painful or pleasurable.

They are:

1. Cognition (प्रमाण)

2. False knowledge (विपर्यय)

3. Fiction (विकल्प)

4. Sleep (निद्रा)

5. Memory (स्मृति)

Note: Cognition consists of knowing or knowledge of something. Yoga psychology calls it pramāṇa. Though Nyāya Darśana calls it pramā, and the means through which the process of pramā (cognition) is accomplished is known in Nyāya as prāmaṇa.

प्रमाकरणं प्रमाणम् ।

pramākaraṇam pramāṇam.

[Meaning] 'Means of pramā is known as pramāṇa.'

तन्निवृत्तावुपशान्तोपरागः स्वस्थः ॥ ३४ ॥

tannivṛttāvupaśāntoparāgaḥ svasthaḥ ॥ 34 ॥

(tannivṛttau) When these vṛttis (states) of the mind cease to function, (upaśāntarāgaḥ) the soul is released from the conditioning of objects of senses of perception and (svasthaḥ) is established in its true nature.

कुसुमवच्च मणिः ॥ ३५ ॥

kusumavachcha maṇiḥ ॥ 35 ॥

(vat cha) Just as (maṇiḥ) a crystal appears red or white (kusumvat cha) in consequence of the proximity of a flower, but on the removal of the same, it assumes its true nature.

The operation of senses causes pain to the soul, then why do they operate? The answer is:

पुरुषार्थं करणोद्भवोऽप्यदृष्टोल्लासात् ॥ ३६ ॥

puruṣārthaṁ karaṇodbhavo'pyadṛṣṭollāsāt ॥ 36 ॥

(karaṇodbhavaḥ) The senses become operational (puruṣārtham) for the sake of the soul (adṛṣṭollāsāt) spontaneously by the grace of kārmic sanskāras of the concerned individual.

धेनुवद्वत्साय ॥ ३७ ॥

dhenuvaddatsāya ॥ 37 ॥

(dhenuvat) Just as milk is spontaneously secreted by the cow (vatsāya) for the sake of the calf.

Now, the question arises as to how many senses are there. The answer is:

करणं त्रयोदशविधमवान्तरभेदात् ॥ ३८ ॥

karaṇaṁ chayodaśavidhamavāntarabhedāt ॥ 38 ॥

(trayodaśavidham) There are 13 types of (karaṇam) senses (avāntara-bhedāt) because of their sub-divisions.

NB: There is one principal sense called mahat (buddhi or intelligence). It is further subdivided into ahaṅkāra, mind, five senses of perception and five senses of action.

If there is one principal sense and others are its sub-divisions, then why do we call them also sense? The answer is:

इन्द्रियेषु साधकतमत्त्वगुणयोगात्कुठारवत् ॥ ३९ ॥

indriyeṣu sādhakatamattvaguṇayogātkuṭhāravat ॥ *39* ॥

(idriyeṣu sādhakatamattvaguṇa-yogāt) Although secondary senses (mind, five senses of perception, and five senses of action) cannot operate without buddhi, they act as immediate means for Buddhi to reach out to external objects, also called senses. (kuṭhāravat) For example, an axe cannot operate itself without an external force for cleaving timber, but that is an immediate means of cleaving timber, so the same is also called a means of cleaving.

Among the eleven senses mentioned above, the mind is called the internal sense, and the other ten are called external senses. Now the question arises: Do all internal and external senses enjoy equal status or otherwise? The answer is:

द्वयोः प्रधानं मनो लोकवद्भृत्यवर्गेषु ॥ ४० ॥

dvayoḥ pradhānaṁ mano lokavadbhṛtyavargeṣu ॥ *40* ॥

Between the two—internal and external group of senses, the internal sense, the mind is the chief sense, and others are subordinate to it, like various servants are subservient to a head servant.

NB: The mind is the chief sense; it collects information from the external senses subordinate to it and passes it on to Buddhi.

अव्यभिचारात् ॥ ४१ ॥

avyabhichārāt ॥ *41* ॥

(avyabhichārāt) The mind is indispensable for each external sense because external senses cannot operate without the mind. This proves that the mind is the chief sense.

तथाशेषसंस्काराधारत्वात् ॥ ४२ ॥

tathāśeṣasaṁskārādhāratvāt ॥ 42 ॥

(tathā aśeṣasanskārādhāratvāt) Mind also stores all sanskāras [information gathered by external senses from the outside world]. This also makes the mind head of all external senses.

स्मृत्यानुमानाच्च ॥ ४३ ॥

smṛtyānumānāchcha ॥ 43 ॥

The Preeminence of the mind is also inferred from smṛti vṛtti [memory function] of the mind, as memory in the mind is created based upon the stored information supplied by external senses to the mind.

Now, the question arises: what motivates the activation of the senses? Do they activate by self-motivation for the bhoga and mokṣa of the soul, or due to some other factor? The answer is:

संभवेन्न स्वतः ॥ ४४ ॥

sambhavenna svataḥ ॥ 44 ॥

(svataḥ) Self-motivation (na) is not (sambavet) possible because the senses are made of matter, and material things cannot become active because of self-motivation. They need external force for the action/motion. As such, the senses are activated by the the desire of the soul.

आपेक्षिको गुणप्रधानभावः क्रियाविशेषात् ॥ ४५ ॥

āpekṣiko guṇapradhānabhāvaḥ kriyāviśeṣāt ॥ 45 ॥

(guṇa-pradhāna-bhāvaḥ) The condition of secondary and principal senses is (āpekṣikaḥ) relative (kriyāviśeṣāt) on account of the difference in their functions. For example, external senses can do only one particular function; one cannot perform the function of another, but the mind can perform the function of all senses, so the mind is principal, and other senses are secondary. Concerning the function of eyes and other senses [each performing one function], the mind (performing multifunctions) is principal, and vice versa; about the function of the mind, other senses are secondary. Similarly, based on information supplied by the mind, Buddhi makes decisions, so Buddhi is principal in relation to the mind, and the mind is secondary in relation to the Buddhi.

Now the question arises, why all senses work for the soul in achieving bhoga and mokṣa? The answer is:

तत्कर्मार्जितत्वात्तदर्थमभिचेष्टालोकवत् ॥ ४६ ॥

tatkarmārjitatvāttadarthamabhicheṣṭā lokavat ॥ 46 ॥

(tat-karmārjitatvāt) Since all these senses are acquired by the soul through its karmas (tadarthamabhichestā), they work for the soul. (lokavat) In worldly affairs, we experience that an instrument purchased by a particular person will always be at his disposal.

समानकर्मयोगे बुद्धेः प्राधान्यं लोकवल्लोकवत् ॥ ४७ ॥

samānakarmayoge buddheḥ prādhānyaṁ lokavallokavat ॥47 ॥

(samāna-karmayoge) Although all internal and external senses work together to help the soul achieve bhoga and mokṣa (buddheḥ prādhānyam), buddhi gets credit. (lokavat) As in worldly affairs, the head receives the credit for the work jointly executed by his team.

Third Chapter

In the second chapter, the purpose of the origin of the body, the thirteen senses and tanmātras have been described in detail. In this chapter, the five gross elements of the body, two types of bodies, and the journey of the soul in different species will be explained in detail.

अविशेषाद्विशेषारम्भः ॥ १ ॥

aviśeṣādviśeṣārambhaḥ ॥ 1 ॥

Prakṛti, mahat, ahaṅkāra, and tanmātras [mind, five sensations of perception, five sensations of action] are categorised as aviśeṣa. Viśeṣas are the entities that can be perceived by sense organs with or without the help of material instruments. On the other hand, aviśeṣas are entities that cannot be perceived by sense organs with or without the help of material instruments. To sum up aviśeṣas do not reflect the viśeṣatā [quality] of the world. What is the quality of the world? To be perceived by the sense organs is the quality of the world or the objects of the world.

So it is said that (aviśeṣāt) The aviśeṣas [buddhi, ahaṅkāra, mind, sensations of perception, and sensations of action jointly called liṅga śarīra] (ārambaḥ) give rise to (viśeṣa) viśeṣas like sensory organs and motor organs.

तस्माच्छरीरस्य ॥ २ ॥

tasmāchchharīrasya ॥ 2 ॥

(tasmāt) From these viśeṣas [five sense organs and motor organs] (śarīrasya), the bodies of souls (first evolving in zygotes) are formed.

तद्बीजात्संसृतिः ॥ ३ ॥

tadbījātsaṁsṛtiḥ ॥ 3 ॥

(tadbījāt) As per seed [sanskāras] (sansṛti) souls move from one body to another body of various species.

Now the question arises: how long does the formation process of bodies of various species from tanmātras continue? The answer is as follows:

आ विवेकाच्च प्रवर्तनमविशेषाणाम् ॥ ४ ॥

āvivekāchcha pravartanamaviśeṣāṇām ॥ 4 ॥

(cha) And (aviśeṣāṇām) Prakṛti and its aviśeṣa products [mahat, ahaṅkāra, mind, sensations of perception and sensations of action] (pravartanam) continue to form bodies for the souls (āvivekāt) till the time they realise their true nature.

उपभोगादितरस्य ॥ ५ ॥

upabhogāditarasya ॥ 5 ॥

The formation of bodies by the Prakṛti and its aviśeṣa products continues (itarasya) for those souls that fail to realise their true nature (upabhogāt) because they will have to reap the fruits of their karmas.

संप्रति परिमुक्तो द्वाभ्याम् ॥ ६ ॥

samprati parimuktā dvābhyām ॥ 6 ॥

(samprati) During the creation phase, souls (parimuktaḥ) are embraced (dvābhyām) by sanskāras of dharma and adharma.

Note: Dharma represents moral and ethical values, right knowledge, sāttvika food habits, and work and conduct. Opposite it is adhārmika [tāmasika habits, work, and conduct].

NB: Pari+mukta = bound or embraced

Jīvana+mukta= living liberated

मातापितृजं स्थूलं प्रायश इतरन्न तथा ॥ ७ ॥

mātāpitṛjaṁ sthūlaṁ prāyaśa itaranna tathā ॥ 7 ॥

(sthūlam) The sexually produced physical body (prāyaśaḥ) usually arises (mātā-pitṛjam) from the sperm of the father and the ovum of the mother; (itarat) Asexually produced other bodies like that of trees, plants, insects, and micro-organisms (na) are not formed (tathā) like this [sperm and ovum of parents].

पूर्वोत्पत्तेस्तत्कार्यत्वं भोगादेकस्य नेतरस्य ॥ ८ ॥

pūrvotpattestatkāryatvaṁ bhogādekasya netarasya ॥ 8 ॥

(tatkāryatvam) The gross material body is the product (pūrvotpatteḥ) of the subtle body that arose first (bhogāt) because the bhoga of pleasure and pain is experienced (ekasya) by one [subtle body], (na) not (itarasya) by the other [gross body].

सप्तदशैकं लिङ्गम् ॥ ९ ॥

saptadaśaikam liṅgam ॥ 9 ॥

(liṅgam) Subtle body (saptadaśa+ekam) comprises of seventeen plus one, i.e. eighteen elements.

NB: Buddhi, Ahaṅkāra, Mind, five tanmātras, five senses of perception and five senses of action together known as liṅga śarīra. This liṅga śarīra is also called vijñāna or vijñānamaya koṣa (buddhi and its sub-divisions).

All souls have the same senses as their liṅga śarīra, but still, species are distinct. This issue is addressed in the next sūtra.

व्यक्तिभेदः कर्मविशेषात् ॥ १० ॥

vyaktibhedaḥ karmaviśeṣāt ॥ 10 ॥

(karmaviśeṣāt) The particular kārmika sanskāras of souls (vyakti-bhedaḥ) cause the distinction in species. Because diverse species are required to reap the fruits of diverse karmas.

How the term body applied only to the gross physical body and not to the subtle body?

तदधिष्ठानाश्रये देहे तद्वादात्तद्वादः ॥ ११ ॥

tadadhiṣṭhānāśraye dehe tadvādāttadvādaḥ ॥ 11 ॥

(tadadhiṣṭhāna) The subtle body is the soul's residence, and (dehe) the gross physical body (āśraye) shelters the subtle body. (tadvādāt) Since the gross physical body is called 'body' (tadvādaḥ), so the subtle body, being sheltered by the gross body, is also called the body.

न स्वातन्त्र्यात्तद्दृते छायावच्चित्रवच्च ॥ १२ ॥

na svātantrayāttadṛte chhāyāvachchitravachcha ॥ 12 ॥

A subtle body made of senses (na) cannot exist (svātantrayāt) independently (tadṛte) without the support of the gross body (chhāyāvat) as there can be no shadow without physical object which intercepts light, (cha) and (chitravat) a picture also requires a physical object to support it.

The question arises: the subtle body made of senses is the effect [product] of Prakṛti, so it has a material form. Why cannot it exist independently? The answer is:

मूर्त्तत्वेऽपि न सङ्घातयोगात्तरणिवत् ॥ १३ ॥

mūrttatvepi na saṅghātayogāttaraṇivat ॥ 13 ॥

Although the subtle body has a material form, being the product of Prakṛti [matter], it cannot exist without an organised material structure like the physical body. For example, light, though material, is not visible. It can only be seen when blocked by a material object and reflected.

Hereunder, the size of liṅgaśarīra variously called Vijñāna, Buddhi, or Mind is mentioned.

अणुपरिमाणं तत्कृतिश्रुतेः ॥ १४ ॥

aṇuparimāṇaṁ tatkṛtiśruteḥ ॥ 14 ॥

The subtle body called vijñāna or mind is (aṇu-parimāṇam) of atomic size, (tatkṛtiśruteḥ) as the Vedic texts talk about its motion. For example, the *Bṛhadāraṇyaka Up.* (4.4.2) mentions:

तमुत्क्रामन्तं प्राणोऽनुत्क्रामति प्राणमनुत्क्रामन्तं स विज्ञानो भवति ।

tamutkrāmantaṁ prāṇo'nutkrāmati prāṇamanutkrāmantaṁ sa vijñāno bhavati ।

[Meaning] When the soul leaves the gross physical body, prāṇas [vital airs] also leave it; when prāṇas do not leave the gross physical body, it is reduced in the subtle body. When prāṇas leaves the gross physical body, it becomes dead [non-functional], and only the subtle body comprised of Buddhi and its subdivisions [colectively called mind] survives.

Similarly, the *Taittirīya Upaniṣad* (2.5.1) speaks of vijñāna [liṅga śarīra] as under:

विज्ञानं यज्ञं तनुते । कर्माणि तनुतेऽपि च । विज्ञानं देवाः सर्वे । ब्रह्म ज्येष्ठमुपासते ॥

vijñānaṁ yajñaṁ tanute / karmāṇi tanute'pi ca /vijñānaṁ devāḥ sarve /brahma jyeṣṭhamupāsate /

[Meaning] Vijñāna [sanskāras stored in the Cosmic Buddhi or mind of Brahman called Prakṛti] causes the extension of yajña [process of creation]. Vijñāna [sanskāras accumulated in Buddhi or mind of Jīvas] is the cause of actions done by them. All enlightened persons, having developed their vijñānamaya koṣa, meditate upon Brahman in Samādhi.

Liṅga śarīra is also indirectly nourished by food consumed by the gross physical body directly.

तदन्नमयत्वश्रुतेश्च ॥ १५ ॥

tadannamayatvaśruteścha ॥ *15* ॥

According to (śruteḥ) the statement of Vedic texts, (tad) liṅga śarīra is (annamayatva) indirectly nourished by food consumed by the gross physical body directly.

The Chhandogya Up. (6.5.4) says:

अन्नमय हि सोम्य मन आपोमयः प्राणस्तेजोमयी वागिति भूय एव मा भगवान्विज्ञापयत्विति तथा सोम्येति होवाच ॥

annamaya hi somya mana āpomayaḥ prāṇastejomayī vāgiti bhūya eva mā bhagavānvijñāpayatviti tathā somyeti hovāca॥

[Meaning] "Thus, my dear, the mind is nourished by food consumed by the gross physical body. Water consumed by the physical body nourishes the prāṇas (vital airs), and the heat of the physical body nourishes the power of speech" "Please, venerable Sir, instruct me further." "So be it, my dear."

Why does this liṅga śarīra made of matter get transferred from one body to another body? The answer is given in the next sūtra.

पुरुषार्थं संसृतिर्लिङ्गानां सूपकारवद्राज्ञः ॥ १६ ॥

puruṣārtham saṁsṛtirliṅgānāṁ sūpakāravadrājñaḥ ॥ *16* ॥

Liṅga śarīra of a soul (sansṛti) keeps on transferring along with the soul from one body to another body (purūṣārtham) to facilitate the soul with the material of bhoga and mokṣa (sūpakāravat rājñaḥ) like the cook of a king accompanies him from one place to another place to facilitate him with sweet dishes.

Having discussed the characteristics of the subtle body, the author now discusses the characteristics of the gross physical body.

पाञ्चभौतिको देहः ॥ १७ ॥

pāñchabhautiko dehaḥ ॥ 17 ॥

(dehaḥ) This gross physical body is (pāñchabhautikaḥ) made of five evolutes (elements).

चातुर्भौतिकमित्येके ॥ १८ ॥

Chāturbhautikam ityeke ॥ 18 ॥

(eke) Some say that (chāturbhautikam) it is made up of four evolutes.

ऐकभौतिकमित्यपरे ॥ १९ ॥

aikabhautikamityapare ॥ 19 ॥

(apare) Others say that (aikabhautikam) it is a product of one evolute (earth).

न सांसिद्धिकं चैतन्यं प्रत्येकादृष्टेः ॥ २० ॥

na sāṁsiddhikam chaitanyam pratyekādṛṣṭeḥ ॥ 20 ॥

(chaitanyam) life is (adṛṣṭeḥ) not seen (pratyeka) in any of the five evolutes, so this physical body made up of five evolutes is (na sānsiddhikam) lifeless by nature.

प्रपञ्चमरणाद्यभावश्च ॥ २१ ॥

prapañchamaraṇādyabhāvaścha ॥ 21 ॥

Had the five evolutes and the physical body been endowed with life by nature, (prapañcha maraṇādi) the physical body and other material things made up of five evolutes (abhāvaḥ) would have never died.

One may say that each evolute doesn't need to be full of life, but life emerges when more than one evolute is compounded. The answer is given below:

मदशक्तिवच्चेत्प्रत्येक परिदृष्टे सांहत्ये तदुद्भवः ॥ २२ ॥

madaśaktivachchetpratyeka paridṛṣṭe sāṁhatye tadudbhavaḥ ॥ 22 ॥

(Chet) If you say that life emerges from the compound of evolutes [or from the arrangement and bonding of atoms of matter], (madśakti-vat) like intoxicating power remerges when two substances are mixed up or arranged, (tadudbhavaḥ) life could have emerged (pratyeka) in each (sāṁhatye) compounded substance (paridṛṣṭe) that comes to our notice.

It was stated that liṅga śarīra transfers along with its soul from one body to another body to facilitate the soul with the material of bhoga and mokṣa. Hereunder, the author is going to tell about the stage of mokṣa.

ज्ञानान्मुक्तिः ॥ २३ ॥

jñānānmuktiḥ ॥ 23 ॥

(muktiḥ) Mokṣa is attained (jñānāt) on the realisation of discrimination between material body and soul [self-realisation or viveka].

बन्धो विपर्ययात् ॥ २४ ॥

bandho viparyayāt ॥ 24 ॥

Non-realisation of the discrimination between the soul and the material body is the cause of bondage.

नियतकारणत्वान्न समुच्चयविकल्पौ ॥ २५ ॥

niyatakāraṇatvānna samuchchayavikalpau ॥ 25 ॥

(niyat-kāraṇatvāt) Self-realisation is the exclusive and precise cause of mokṣa. (na samuchchaya-vikalpau) No other cause [like sāttvika deed] is required together with self-realisation to achieve mokṣa. There is no alternate cause for mokṣa.

Clubbing some other work with self-realisation is like clubbing the dreaming and waking states. The illustration is given below:

स्वप्रजागराभ्यामिव मायिकामायिकाभ्यां नोभयोर्मुक्तिः पुरुषस्य ॥ २६ ॥

svaprajāgarābhyāmiva māyikāmāyikābhyāṁ nobhayormuktiḥ
puruṣasya ॥ 26 ॥

(iva) For instance, (svapna-jāgarābhyām) dreaming and waking states are two different states; they cannot be clubbed together and exist together because of their different natures. (māyika-amāyikābhyām) The dream state is unreal, and the waking state is real. Similarly, (ubhayoḥ) clubbing some other work with the work of self-realisation (na) is not going to help a (puruṣasya) person (muktiḥ) in mokṣa.

इतरस्यापि नात्यन्तिकम् ॥ २७ ॥

itarasyāpi nātyantikam ॥ 27 ॥

If knowledge of Prakṛti is taken as an option or alternative to self-realisation, that will not help mitigate the suffering permanently [achieve mokṣa].

संकल्पितेऽप्येवम् ॥ २८ ॥

saṁkalpite'pyevam ॥ 28 ॥

(saṅkalpite api evam) Merely accumulation of sanskāras [information] of mokṣa in mind is not going to solve the problem.

भावनोपचयाच्छुद्धस्य सर्वं प्रकृतिवत्॥ २९ ॥

bhāvanopachayāchchhuddhasya sarvaṁ Prakṛtivat ‖ *29* ‖

(bhāvanā-upachayāt) Observance of bhāvanā sanskāra [sañyama] in Prakṛti (śuddhasya) by a purified mind [sāttvika] leads him/her (sarvam) to enjoy all powers (Prakṛti-vat) like that of Prakṛti, such as materialising anything instantly, but those powers attained through sañyama in Prakṛti are not going to help in mokṣa. Only self-realisation is the way out.

Note: Becoming one with Prakṛti in samādhi is sañyama.

Having established that self-realisation is the exclusive means of mokṣa, the means of self-realisation are described hereunder:

रागोपहतिर्ध्यानम् ॥ ३० ॥

rāgopahatirdhyānam ‖ *30* ‖

Dhāraṇā [focused attention], Dhyāna [meditation] and Samādhi are the primary means of self-realisation. Attachment to worldly objects is the greatest obstacle in perfecting dhyāna, etc. Success in perfecting (dhyānam), dhyāna, etc., can be achieved (rāgaopahati) by removing attachment from worldly objects.

How to succeed in detachment?

वृत्तिनिरोधात्तत्सिद्धिः ॥ ३१ ॥

vṛttinirodhāttatsiddhiḥ ‖ *31* ‖

(tatsiddhiḥ) Perfection in dhyāna, etc. can be achieved (vṛtti-nirodhāt) by withdrawal of mind [attention] from the outside world.

धारणासनस्वकर्मणा तत्सिद्धिः ॥ ३२ ॥

dhāraṇāsanasvakarmaṇā tatsiddhiḥ ॥ 32 ॥

(tatsiddhiḥ) Success in withdrawal of mind [attention] can be achieved by constant practice of (dhāraṇā) internal attention or focus, (āsana) proper posture, and (svakarmaṇā) performing duties prescribed by Śāstra for one's Āśrama [Brahmacharya, Gṛhastha, Vānaprastha and Saṃnyāsa].

निरोधश्छर्दिविधारणाभ्याम् ॥ ३३ ॥

nirodhaśchhardividhāraṇābhyām ॥ 33 ॥

Perfection in dhāraṇā [focused attention] can be achieved through perfection of breath which can further be achieved by prāṇāyāma [regulating (chhardi) external and (vidhāraṇa) internal breathings].

Note: Control of mind is possible through controlling breath.

Having explained dhāraṇā [focused attention of mind], now āsana is explained.

स्थिरसुखमासनम् ॥ ३४ ॥

sthirasukhamāsanam ॥ 34 ॥

(āsanam) Āsana is a (sthira-sukham) steady and comfortable posture.

Now, sva-karma is defind.

स्वकर्म स्वाश्रमविहितकर्मानुष्ठानम् ॥ ३५ ॥

svakarma svāśramavihitakarmānuṣṭhānam ॥ 35 ॥

(svakarma) Svakarma means (anuṣṭhānam) performing (karma) duties (vihita) prescribed by Śāstra (svāśrama) for one's own Āśrama [Brahmacharya, Gṛhastha, Vānaprastha and Saṃnyasa].

वैराग्यादभ्यासाच्च ॥ ३६ ॥

vairāgyādabhyāsāchcha ॥ *36* ॥

(abhyāsāt) Constant practice of dhyāna, etc., (cha) and (vairāgyāt) detachment is helpful in self-realisation.

विपर्ययभेदाः पञ्च ॥ ३७ ॥

viparyayabhedāḥ pañcha ॥ *37* ॥

(pañcha) There are five (viparyaya-bhedāḥ) types of Viparyaya (False knowledge)

1. Avidyā: Avidyā is the sense of permanence in the transient, of purity in the impure, of pleasure in the painful, of soul in the matter.

2. Asmitā: Asmitā is the identification of the seer [soul] with the material instrument of the seeing [eyes]. The soul is the seer, and eyes are the material instruments of seeing, so considering eyes as a seer [soul] is asmitā.

3. Rāga: Once having gone through a pleasurable experience, the desire to seek the pleasure again is called Rāga or attachment.

4. Dveṣa: After a painful experience, the arousal of aversion to pain is known as dveṣa.

5. Abhiniveśa: The natural fear of death which prevails upon learned and laity alike is called abhiniveśa.

अशक्तिरष्टाविंशतिधा तु ॥ ३८ ॥

aśaktiraṣṭāviṁśatidhā tu ॥ *38* ॥

Viparyaya (aśaktir-aṣṭāviṁśatidhā) disables twenty-eight types of powers. The list of powers disabled by viparyaya is—

11 powers of 11 senses, nine powers arising out of perfection of tuṣṭi [contentment] and eight divine powers attained in the course of doing yogābhāsa [practice of yoga].

तुष्टिर्नवधा ॥ ३९ ॥

tuṣṭirnavadhā ॥ *39* ॥

Tuṣṭi [contentment] is of nine types.

सिद्धिरष्टधा ॥ ४० ॥

siddhirastadhā ॥ *40* ॥

Divine powers attained through yoga during the attempt at self-realisation are called siddhis. There are eight types of siddhis.

1. Aṇimā: Reduction of the body to the level of atom.

2. Laghimā: Becoming light.

3. Mahimā: Becoming very large.

4. Prāpti: Access to all places, even touching the moon sitting on the surface of the earth.

5. Garimā: Becoming very heavy.

6. Through sañyama on the nature of bhūtas, a yogī attains the siddhi (divine power) of Prakāmya, i.e. a yogī can enter everything at will, even into the earth like that of waters.

7. Through sañyama on the subtle (atomic) form of bhūtas, a yogī attains the siddhi (divine power) of Vaśitva, i.e. control over all material things and other living beings, including gross bhūtas. However, a yogī is free from the control of everything.

8. Through sañyama on Anvaya, a yogī attains the siddhi (divine power) of Īśitva, i.e. a yogī attains the power of

creation and destruction of all material objects.

अवान्तरभेदाः पूर्ववत् ॥ ४१ ॥

avāntarabhedāḥ pūrvavat ॥ *41* ॥

(pūrvavat) According to its five aforementioned divisions, (avāntara-bhedāḥ) Viparyaya can further be subdivided. For example,

1. Avidyā (sense of soul in the matter): There are eight material elements starting from Prakṛti to its seven vikṛtis like buddhi (cosmic mind), ahaṅkāra (individuality), and five tanmātras (guṇas of five bhūtas). To consider all eight material things as souls makes Avidyā of eight types.

2. Asmitā [identification of oneself [soul] with the material elements]: Asmitā can also be subdivided into eight types if a soul identifies itself with the eight material elements cited above.

3. Rāga [the desire to seek pleasure from sensory objects]: There are five sensory objects. They are śabda [sound], sparśa [touch], rūpa [sight], rasa [taste] and gandha [smell]. These five objects can be categorised into two types: divya [divine] and adivya [normal]. Whatever is perceived by yogis with divine powers is called divya, and whatever is perceived by a normal human being is called adivya [normal]. Thus rāga can be subdivided into ten types from the point of five divya and five adivya sensory objects.

4. Dveṣa [aversion to sensory material elements and sensory objects]: There are eight material elements and ten sensory objects, as discussed above. So, dveṣa can be subdivided into 18 types.

5. Abhiniveśa [fear of death]: The fear of one's death with the destruction of the above-mentioned 18 bases of dveṣa makes abhiniveśa of 18 subtypes.

Thus, there are 62 subdivisions of Viparyaya.

एवमितरस्याः ॥ ४२ ॥

evamitarasyāḥ ॥ *42* ॥

(evam) So should be understood (itarasyāḥ) the twenty-eight sub-divisions of aśakti [disability], which is already explained in sūtra thirty eight above.

आध्यात्मिकादिभेदान्नवधा तुष्टिः ॥ ४३ ॥

ādhyātmikādibhedānnavadhā tuṣṭiḥ ॥ *43* ॥

(ādhyātmikādibhedāt) From the point of adhyātma and others, (tuṣṭiḥ) tuṣṭi [contentment] has (navadhā) nine subdivisions.

There are four ādhyātmika tuṣṭis [subjective contentments].

1. Prakṛti (Matter): Whatever changes are happening on the way to self-realisation, they are caused by Prakṛti; I am indifferent and have no role in these happenings. To remain contended with this thought is called Prakṛti Tuṣṭi. Another name of Prakṛti in the Vedas is Ambha. So this tuṣṭi is also called Ambhas Tuṣṭi. If a seeker remains contended with this thought and do not intervene for the progress of his spiritual elevation, he never achieves the goal of self-realisation.

2. Upādāna [Means]: After wearing rudrākṣa beads, holding daṇḍa [rod] and kamaṇḍalu [water pot made of a dry gourd. i.e. pumpkin or coconut shell, metal, wood or clay] and initiation into saṁnyāsa, if a seeker

becomes contended that now he will attain self-realisation, this notion is known as Upādāna Tuṣṭi or Salila Tuṣṭi. By this notion, he is not going to attain self-realisation until he makes appropriate efforts to achieve it.

3. Kāla [Time]: After taking saṁnyāsa and observing a little bit dhyāna [meditation] for some period, if a seeker thinks that mokṣa will not result from his/her efforts but will come in due course of time, this notion is called Kāla Tuṣṭi or Ogha Tuṣṭi. He can never attain self-realisation without delving deep into various forms of Samādhi.

4. Bhāgya (Luck): Even by force of time, not all attain mokṣa, but only by good luck can one attain mokṣa; this type of notion is called Bhāgya Tuṣṭi. It is also called Vṛṣṭi Tuṣṭi.

The four tuṣṭis mentioned above are called subjective tuṣṭis as they depend upon the subjective opinion of the seeker.

The following five tuṣṭis are objective tuṣṭis, since they are caused by the abstinence from sensory objects.

5. Arjana (acquisition of material objects), 6. Rakṣaṇa (preservation of material things), 7. Kṣaya (transitoriness), 8. Bhoga (consumption of worldly resources), and 9. Hinsā (violence): When a seeker abstains from all the above because he/she is fed up with them given the evils involved. These are a total of 9 tuṣṭis. A seeker is wrong if he thinks that abstaining from these nine tuṣṭis will help him in self-realisation. Apart from these tuṣṭis, he had to put further efforts like perfection in dhāraṇā, dhyāna and samādhi to attain the

goal of self-realisation.

ऊहादिभिः सिद्धिः ॥ ४४ ॥

ūhādibhiḥ siddhiḥ ॥ 44 ॥

Those eight divine powers are achieved employing Ūha [reasoning as to what God is, what the soul is and how we do attain self realisation] and others (like Śabda [oral instructions of expert Guru], Adhyayana [study of Śāstras], *Ādhyātmika duḥkha vighāta* [control over pains related to the body and mind through spiritual elevation], *Ādhidaivika duḥkha vighāta* [control over pains caused by natural calamities], *Ādhibhautika duḥkha vighāta* [control over pains caused by humans, others and material objects], Suhṛtprāpti [blessed with a friend who can guide him the path of self-realisation] and Dāna [charity done with a sense of duty to a deserving person who is not able to repay for it at the right place and time].

Note: These fifty factors [9 tuṣṭis, eight siddhis, five viparyayas and 28 aśaktis] are obstacles in self-realisation. Proper control over them leads to self-realisation. This is explained in the next sutra.

नेतरादितरहानेन विना ॥ ४५ ॥

netarāditarahānena vinā ॥ 45 ॥

Until the time (itara-hānena vinā) these fifty factors are controlled (itarāt) with the help of Ūha and others, one cannot attain self-realisation.

Attainment of bhogas and mokṣa is possible in the creation. So, having explained the way of attaining self-realisation or mokṣa, various forms of creation are explained forthwith.

दैवादिप्रभेदा ॥ ४६ ॥

daivādiprabhedā ॥ 46 ॥

(daivādi-prabhedā) The creation is broadly classified into three categories: Daiva [natural], Tiryak [species below human beings] and Mānuṣa [human beings].

Daiva-creation is further divided into eight sub-categories— like Brāhma [creation of supergalactic centre], Prājāpatya [creation of galaxies], Aindra [creation of stars], Paitrya [creation of satellites], Gāndharva [creation of planets], Yākṣa [creation of non-pathogenic bacteria], Rākṣasa [creation of pathogenic bacteria] and Paiśācha [creation of viruses].

Tiryak-creation has five sub-categories— like Paśu [domestic animals], Mṛga [wild animals], Pakṣī [birds], Sarīsṛpa [reptiles and others] and Sthāvara [trees, plants, herbs and shrubs etc.].

Mānuṣa-creation has no sub-category. Class of human beings is one.

आब्रह्मस्तम्बपर्यन्तं तत्कृते सृष्टिराविवेकात् ॥ ४७ ॥

ābrahmastambaparyantaṁ tatkṛte sṛṣṭirāvivekāt ॥ 47 ॥

(ābrahma-stambaparyantam) From the super-galactic centre to trees and plants, (sṛṣṭiḥ) the whole creation is (tatkṛte) for the bhoga and mokṣa of the souls (āvivekāt) till they attain self-realisation.

What will be the fate of a soul till it attains mokṣa? The same is explained below:

ऊर्ध्वं सत्त्वविशाला ॥ ४८ ॥

ūrdhvaṁ sattvaviśālā ॥ 48 ॥

(sattva-viśālā) Souls endowed with sattva-guṇa-sanskāras are born (ūrdhvam) as divine beings [high profile yogīs]. This is called Svarga loka [heaven] in Vedic technical terms.

तमोविशाला मूलतः ॥ ४९ ॥

tamoviśālā mūlataḥ ॥ 49 ॥

(tamoviśālā) Souls endowed with tamoguṇa-sanskāras are born (mūlataḥ) in tiryaka [species lower than a human being] species. Lower species like trees, animals, birds, and insects are called Naraka loka or hell in Vedic technical terms.

मध्ये रजोविशाला ॥ ५० ॥

madhye rajoviśālā ॥ 50 ॥

(rajoviśālā) Souls endowed with rajoguṇa-sanskāras are born (madhye) as human beings (sandwiched between high-profile yogīs and Tiryaka [animals and others] species.

कर्मवैचित्र्यात्प्रधानचेष्टा गर्भदासवत् ॥ ५१ ॥

karmavaichitrayātpradhānacheṣṭā garbhadāsavat ॥ 51 ॥

(karmavaichitryāt) Because of the variety of kārmic sanskāras of souls, (pradhāna cheṣṭā) Prakṛti behaves in variegated ways to produce a variety of suitable bodies for the souls (garbha-dāśavat), like slavery is reflected in the natural behaviour of a born slave [a person born with sanskāras of slavery].

When owing to one's karmas, a person can go to higher species [daiva species], then what need is there for mokṣa? To this, the author replies:

आवृत्तिस्तत्राप्युत्तरोत्तरयोनियोगाद्धेयः ॥ ५२ ॥

āvṛttistatrāpyuttarottarayoniyogāddheyaḥ ॥ 52 ॥

(uttarottara-yoni-yogāt) Even when higher and higher [animal to man and man to divinity or high profile yogī] species are attained by a soul because of the purity of its karmas, (āvṛttiḥ) there is a return (tatra) to the human body [i.e. a soul cannot get rid of human life], because in the state of divinity [high profile yogī], a soul continues to occupy a human body. Therefore, mokṣa is required (heyaḥ) to abandon the human life.

The author further emphasis the need of mokṣa.

समानं जरामरणादिजं दुःखम् ॥ ५३ ॥

samānaṁ jarāmaraṇādijaṁ duḥkham ॥ *53* ॥

Mokṣa is required, as souls in all species have equal pain of old age and death. Whatever pain of old age and death is felt by a soul in the body of a lower species and the human species, the same pain is felt by a soul in the life of a high- profile yogī because of occupation to the human body. So, the necessity of mokṣa is emphasised.

One may raise a question that after death, the material body is absorbed into its cause Prakṛti, so why not this absorption of body [effect] into its cause [Prakṛti] be considered mokṣa? To this, the author replies.

न कारणलयात्कृतकृत्यता मग्नवदुत्थानात् ॥ ५४ ॥

na kāraṇalayātkṛtakṛtyatā magnavadutthānāt ॥ *54* ॥

(kāraṇa-layāt) The absorption of the body into its cause Prakṛti after death (na kṛta-kṛtyatā) cannot be called mokṣa because death is always followed by birth (magnavad utthānāt) as the body of a person dived/ drowned in waters rises again.

Prakṛti is the ultimate material cause of the material

world, as Prakṛti is not caused by any other cause. Then why does the material body [effect] that has merged into its final cause [Prakṛti] rise again? To this, the author replies as follows:

अकार्यत्वेऽपि तद्योगः पारवश्यात् ॥ ५५ ॥

akāryatve'pi tadyogaḥ pāravaśyāt ॥ 55 ॥

(akāryatve api) Though the Prakṛti is not the effect of any cause [or say ultimate material cause], (tadyogaḥ) the material bodies of souls that have merged into Prakṛti rise again (pāravaśyāt) because of the leftover kārmic sanskāras of the souls.

Now the question arises: who knows about the leftover sanskāras of the souls, and how is all this monitored? The reply is given below:

स हि सर्ववित्सर्वकर्ता ॥ ५६ ॥

sa hi sarvavitsarvakartā ॥ 56 ॥

It all is monitored by Īśvara [God], (hi) because (saḥ) Īśvara [God] (sarvavit) knows everything [omniscient], (sarvakartā) and creator all. He monitors things accordingly.

ईदृशेश्वरसिद्धिः सिद्धा ॥ ५७ ॥

īdṛśeśvarasiddhiḥ siddhā ॥ 57 ॥

(idṛśa-Īśvara-siddhiḥ) Thus, the existence of an omniscient, all-creator and controller God (siddhā) is established.

Note: Most ignorant scholars believe that Sāṅkhya does not accept the existence of Īśvara [nirīśvara Sāṅkhya]. Here is a befitting reply to them.

प्रधानसृष्टिः परार्थं स्वतोऽप्यभोक्तृत्वादुष्ट्रकुङ्कुम वहनवत् ॥ ५८ ॥

*pradhānasṛṣṭiḥ parārtham svato'pyabhoktṛtvāduṣṭrakuṅkuma
vahanavat ॥ 58 ॥*

(pradhāna-sṛṣṭiḥ) Material creation is (prārtham) for the benefit of souls (abhoktṛtvāt) because Prakṛti or matter cannot enjoy its creation (svataḥ) itself, (uṣṭra-kuṅkum-vahanavat) such as a camel carries saffron for its master and not for itself.

Now the question arises that Prakṛti [matter] is non-living, how can it act?

अचेतनत्वेऽपि क्षीरवच्चेष्टितं प्रधानस्य ॥ ५९ ॥

achetanatve'pi kṣīravachcheṣṭitam pradhānasya ॥ 59 ॥

(cheṣṭitam) Action in (achetanatve) non-living (pradhānasya) Prakṛti is inspired by the will of Brahman (kṣīravat) as the milk comes forth from the breasts of the mother at her will to feed the baby.

कर्मवद्दृष्टेर्वा कालादेः ॥ ६० ॥

karmavaddṛṣṭervā kālādeḥ ॥ 60 ॥

(karmavat) As the actions done by human beings bear fruits (kālādeḥ) in time under the law of Ṛta inspired by Brahman, similarly, Prakṛti acts under the law of Ṛta.

स्वभावाच्चेष्टितमनभिसंधानाद् भृत्यवत् ॥ ६१ ॥

svabhāvāchcheṣṭitam-anabhisamdhānānt bhṛtyavat ॥ 61 ॥

(svabhāva) Or we can say that this is the inherent sanskāra of Prakṛti introduced in it by Brahman that (cheṣṭitam) it acts by nature (anabhisandhānāt) not in its own interest but in the interest of the soul (bhṛtyavat), like that of a servant who acts in the interest of his master.

कर्माकृष्टेर्वानादितः ॥ ६२ ॥

karmākṛṣṭervānāditaḥ ॥ 62 ॥

(vā) Or one can say that Prakṛti is active (karmākṛṣṭeḥ) because of the force of karmic sanskāras of the souls (anāditaḥ) since eternity.

After describing the creative act of Prakṛti and its causes, that Prakṛti is active for the sake of another [soul]. The author tries to tell the causes for Prakṛti's ceasing to act.

विविक्तबोधात्सृष्टिनिवृत्तिः प्रधानस्य सूदवत्पाके ॥ ६३ ॥

viviktabodhātsṛṣṭinivṛttiḥ pradhānasya sūdavatpāke ॥ 63 ॥

(vivikta-bodhāt) In consequences of the soul's attaining self-realisation, (pradhānasya) Prakṛti (sṛṣṭi-nivṛttiḥ) ceases to act [to create a suitable body for the concerned soul] (sūdavat) like that of the cook (pāke) when cooking has been completed.

Note: Here, one should be clear that Prakṛti ceases to act for those souls that attain mokṣa, not for those still in bondage. In the next sūtra, the same fact is clarified.

इतर इतरवत्तद्दोषात् ॥ ६४ ॥

itara itaravattaddoṣāt ॥ 64 ॥

(itara) The soul in bondage remains in contact with Prakṛti (itaravat) like other souls in bondage (taddoṣāt) because of their Aviveka [non-attaining self-realisation] or until they attain Viveka [self-realisation].

The author describes the nature of mokṣa.

द्वयोरेकतरस्य वौदासीन्यमपवर्गः ॥ ६५ ॥

dayorekatarasya vaudāsīnyam apavargaḥ ॥ 65 ॥

(audāsīnyam) Disjunction both i.e. the Puruṣa [soul] and Prakṛti [body] to one another (vā) or (ekatarasya) of one [Prakṛti] to another [soul] is called Apavarga [Mokṣa].

Here, one thing must be clear: when the soul attains self-realisation, the disjunction of both soul and Prakṛti to one another takes place, as neither soul is attached with Prakṛti nor Prakṛti acts for the sake of the liberated soul. However, Prakṛti does act for those in bondage. The same fact is clarified below:

अन्यसृष्ट्युपरागेऽपि न विरज्यतेप्रबुद्धरज्जुतत्त्वस्यैवोरगः ॥ ६६ ॥

*anyasṛṣṭyuparāge'pi na virajyate prabuddharajjutattva
syaivoragaḥ ॥ 66 ॥*

(anya-sṛṣṭi-uparāge) For the sake of the soul in bondage, Prakṛti (na) does not (virajyate) cease to act, (iva) as is the case with (uragaḥ) the snake, which ceases to be a terror in respect of him/her (prabuddha-rajjutattvasya) who is aware of the truth concerning the rope, compared to the other who mistakes it for a snake.

कर्मनिमित्तयोगाच्च ॥ ६७ ॥

karmanimittayogāchcha ॥ 67 ॥

(karmanimitta-yogāt cha) Or due to the leftover karmas [sanskāras] of the souls in bondage, Prakṛti continues to act.

नैरपेक्ष्येऽपि प्रकृत्युपकारेऽविवेको निमित्तम् ॥ ६८ ॥

nairapekṣaye'pi prakṛtyupakāre'viveko nimittam ॥ 68 ॥

(api) Although Prakṛti, being insentient, (nairapekṣye) does not require Puruṣa [soul], yet (avivekaḥ) Aviveka of Puruṣa [soul] is the (nimittam) motive cause (prakṛtyupakāre) behind Prakṛti's help towards its [soul's] attaining bhoga and mokṣa.

नर्तकीवत्प्रवृत्तस्यापि निवृत्तिश्चारितार्थ्यात् ॥ ६९ ॥

nartakīvatpravṛttasyāpi nivṛttiścāritārthyāt ॥ 69 ॥

Prakṛti's action is not universal, but it is for the sake of Puruṣa [soul], as soon as the (chāritārthyāt) very objective of the soul is achieved, (pravṛttasyāpi nivṛtti) Prakṛti cease to act for the concerned soul, (nartakīvat) like a dancer stops dancing after the objective of dance is achieved.

दोषबोधेऽपि नोपसर्पणं प्रधानस्य कुलवधूवत् ॥ ७० ॥

doṣabodhe'pi nopasarpaṇaṁ pradhānasya kulavadhūvat ॥ 70 ॥

(pradhānasya upasarpaṇam na) Prakṛti ceases to approach the liberated [self-realised] soul, (doṣabodhe api) as if its pain-giving tendency is exposed to the liberated soul, (kulavadhū-vat) like a woman of high family hesitates to approach her husband on exposition of her fault.

नैकान्ततो बन्धमोक्षौपुरुषस्याविवेकाद्दते ॥ ७१ ॥

naikāntato bandhamokṣau puruṣasyāvivekādṛte ॥ 71 ॥

(bandha-mokṣau) Bondage and liberation (na) do not (puruṣasy) belong to the soul (ekāntataḥ) in reality (ṛte) it is only (avivekāt) because of aviveka [mistaking self for body] that the soul comes in bondage and put efforts for liberation.

प्रकृतेराञ्जस्यात्ससङ्गत्वात्पशुवत् ॥ ७२ ॥

prakṛterāñjasyātsasaṅgatvātpaśuvat ॥ 72 ॥

(āñjasyāt) In reality bondage and liberation belong to (prakṛteḥ) Prakṛti. (sasaṅgatvāt) In association with

Prakṛti, the soul gets bound (paśuvat) like a domestic animal in connection with rope.

रूपैः सप्तभिरात्मानं बध्नाति प्रधानं कोशकारवद्विमोचयत्येक रूपेण ॥ ७३ ॥

rūpaiḥ saptabhirātmānaṁ badhnāti pradhānaṁ kośakārava
dvimochayatyeka rūpeṇa ॥ 73 ॥

Dharma [self-discipline, social discipline, duties, knowledge], adharma [want of dharma], jñāna [self-realisation], ajñāna [want of self-realisation], vairāgya [renunciation], avairāgya [want of renunciation], aiśvarya [divine powers] and anaiśvarya [want of divine powers]— these eight notions are born of Prakṛti. (pradhānam) Prakṛti becomes the (badhnāti) cause of bondage for the (ātmānam) soul (saptabhiḥ rupaiḥ) because of seven of them, (eka-rūpeṇa) only one jñāna [self-realisation] alone (vimochayati) causes the liberation of the soul. This is (kośakāravat) like a silkworm wrapped up from all sides by the cage of silk except for one exit point.

If jñāna (self-realisation) is the cause of mokṣa and the other seven are the cause of bondage, then a seeker desiring mokṣa has to abandon the other seven causes of bondage. In this situation, dharma and vairāgya are also to be abandoned, which are not seen as hurdles in self-realisation. This goes opposite to the visible fact. To this, replies the author:

निमित्तत्वमविवेकस्य न दृष्टहानिः ॥ ७४ ॥

nimittatvamavivekasya na dṛṣṭahāniḥ ॥ 74 ॥

(avivekasya) Aviveka [want of self-realisation] is (nimittatvam) the efficient cause of bondage [not dharma and vairāgya]. So, for self-realisation, stress is upon the abandonment of efficient cause [aviveka] and not dharma and vairāgya. (na dṛṣṭahāni) The above argument does not oppose the visible fact that Dharma and Vairāgya are not the hurdles in self-realisation.

After the aviveka is eliminated, how can viveka be gained?

तत्त्वाभ्यासान्नेति नेतीति त्यागाद्विवेकसिद्धिः ॥ ७५ ॥

tattvābhyāsānneti netīti tyāgādvivekasiddhiḥ ॥ 75 ॥

(viveka-siddhiḥ) Viveka [self-realisation] is gained (tyāgāt) through abandonment of the idea that (neti) neither the soul is Prakṛti [matter], (neti) nor is the Prakṛti [matter] soul and (tattvābhyāsāt) constant practice of self-realisation.

Suppose this is the way to attain mokṣa or self-realisation. In that case, all the seekers doing practice under the guidance of one Guru should attain self-realisation simultaneously in one life itself. The author removes the doubt.

अधिकारिप्रभेदान्न नियमः ॥ ७६ ॥

adhikāriprabhedānna niyamaḥ ॥ 76 ॥

Success in self-realisation is subject to the merit of the concerned seeker. So, due to the different merits of different seekers practising under the same Guru, not all need to attain success simultaneously in one life.

Now, a question arises whether a seeker (soul) leaves the material body immediately after self-realisation or after some time interval. The answer is:

बाधितानुवृत्त्या मध्यविवेकतोऽयुपभोगः ॥ ७७ ॥

bādhitānuvṛttyā madhyavivekato'yupabhogaḥ ॥ 77 ॥

(madhya vivekataḥ) During self-realisation, (bādhita

anuvṛttyā) due to the persistence of unrewarded kārmic sanskāras and sanskāra of aham, (upabhogaḥ) a seeker continues to bear the fruits of unrewarded kārmic sanskāras, so he/she cannot leave the material body until all sanskāras are exhausted.

जीवन्मुक्तश्च ॥ ७८ ॥

jīvanmuktaścha ॥ *78* ॥

(cha) And he is called (jīvanmuktaḥ) Jīvanmūkta [living liberated].

The condition in which a seeker remains embodied due to the persistence of unrewarded kārmic sanskāras and sanskāra of aham even after attaining self-realisation is called Jīvanmukti [living liberation]. Śri Kriṣṇa, Rāma and others were Jivanmukta yogīs.

उपदेश्योपदेष्टृत्वात्तत्सिद्धिः ॥ ७९ ॥

upadeśyopadeṣṭṛtvāttatsiddhiḥ ॥ *79* ॥

The state of Jīvana-mukti [living liberation] is (siddhiḥ) proved (upadeṣṭṛtvāt) by the existence of Instructors (upadeśya) of self-realisation because only a person who has experienced self-realisation can instruct self-realisation to others.

श्रुतिश्च ॥ ८० ॥

śrutiścha ॥ *80* ॥

(cha) Even (śrutiḥ) the existence of Vedic texts proves the existence of Jivanmukta [living liberated]. The Vedic texts were composed by none others but living liberated seers.

इतरथान्धपरंपरा ॥ ८१ ॥

itarathāndhaparaṁparā ॥ *81* ॥

(itarathā) Otherwise [had there been no condition of living liberation], there would be the production of literature by pseudo-scholars introducing fundamentalism, superstitions and blind faiths in society.

That was why Maharshi Dayanand Saraswati, a towering Vedic scholar and Social Reformer of 19th century India, emphasised the study of Ārṣa Granthas [literature composed by living liberated seers].

One may ask a question: when all kārmic sanskāras are exhausted, how can there be life? To this, the answer is:

चक्रभ्रमणवद्धृतशरीरः ॥ ८२ ॥

chakrabhramaṇavaddhṛtaśarīraḥ ॥ *82* ॥

All kārmic sanskaras are eliminated, but the sanskāra of aham [individuality] still persists. Due to the persistence of sanskāra of aham, (dhṛta-śarīra) a yogī maintains his body for some time by force of sāttvika karmas performed earlier, (chakra-bhramaṇa-vat) like a potter's wheel maintains its whirling for some time, even when the stick has been removed, due to force given to it previously.

Note: Because of the persistence of sanskāra of aham, a living liberated yogī can maintain his body until the time he wishes to do so by doing sāttvika karmas. When he erases the sanskāra of aham, he will achieve mokṣa called Videha Mukti [liberation after body]. This fact is further explained in the next sūtra.

संस्कारलेशतस्तत्सिद्धिः ॥ ८३ ॥

sanskāraleśatastatsiddhiḥ ॥ *83* ॥

(tatsiddhiḥ) The body can be maintained by a living

liberated yogī (sanskāra leśataḥ) even if a fraction of sanskāra [of aham or sāttvika karmas] is retained.

विवेकान्निःशेषदुःखनिवृत्तौ कृतकृत्यता नेतरान्नेतरात् ॥ ८४ ॥

vivekānniḥśeṣaduḥkhanivṛttau kṛtakṛtyatā netarānnetarāt ॥84 ॥

(niḥśeṣa-duḥkha-nivṛttau) Assuage of all sufferings is possible only (vivekāt) by self-realisation (kṛtakṛtyatā), which is the final objective of human life; it is not possible (netrāt) by any other means (netarāt), by any other means.

Note: Here, repetition marks the end of the chapter.

Fourth Chapter

Having explained self-realisation technically [from the point of Śāstra], in this chapter, the means of self-realisation will be described within the ambit of Śāstra through famous examples prevalent in society.

राजपुत्रवत्तत्त्वोपदेशात् ॥ १ ॥

rājaputravattattvopadeśāt ॥ *1* ॥

Self-realisation can be attained by the concerned seeker (tattvopadeśāt) through the instructions of the expert Guru by recalling that he/she is not body but soul (rājaputravat), as happened in the case of the lost son of the king.

The story goes like this: the son of the king got lost in a jungle in his infancy. He was brought up by foresters. Once, the minister of the king, while moving through the jungle, identified him. The child considered him a forester, but the minister reminded him that he was not a forester but the king's son. The child cast off the idea of his being a forester and betook himself to his true royal state.

Sometimes, a third person also benefits as a consequence of instructions given for the benefit of somebody else. An example is provided in the next sūtra.

पिशाचवदन्यार्थोपदेशेऽपि ॥ २ ॥

piśāchavadanyārthopadeśe'pi ॥ *2* ॥

(piśācha-vat) As the Piśācha was benefitted (upadeśe) from the instructions given (anyārtham api) for the benefit of someone else.

There is a story related to it. Once, a Guru intended to give instructions to his disciples for self-realisation. He took him to the forest in a secluded place and started giving him instructions. A Piśācha [a non-vegetarian person] also came to know about it, and he started overhearing instructions while concealing himself in a place. Thus, the Piśācha also attained self-realisation by overhearing and following the instructions.

आवृत्तिरसकृदुपदेशात् ॥ ३ ॥

āvṛttirasakṛdupadeśāt ॥ *3* ॥

(āvṛttir asakṛt) Repetition of (upadeśāt) instructions will help attain knowledge [self-realisation].

Knowledge [self-realisation] may be attained even by a friend's or relative's instructions. The instructor doesn't need to be a Guru. The example of father and son is given in the next sūtra.

पितापुत्रवदुभयोर्दृष्टत्वात् ॥ ४ ॥

pitāputravadubhayordṛṣṭatvāt ॥ *4* ॥

(ubhayayor dṛṣṭatvāt) Sometimes, it is seen that the instructor and instructed are not qualified Guru and disciples (pitā-putravat) as in the case of father and son.

The story goes like this: a particular person had to send his pregnant wife to her father's house because of poverty. He moved to another country to earn money. He returned home after a long time and, seeing his son, did not recognise him. The mother acquainted her husband and son with one another; hence both could identitfy each other. The moral of the story is that the knowledge of truth may arise even without the instructions of a Guru.

Abandonment of worldly objects [tyāga] plays a vital role in self-realisation. With the growing asceticism [vairāgya], one should strengthen the notion of abandonment. This is advised in the next sūtra.

श्येनवत्सुखदुःखी त्यागवियोगाभ्याम् ॥ ५ ॥

śyenavatsukhaduḥkhī tyāgaviyogābhyām ॥ 5 ॥

(śyenavat) Like the hawk (sukha-duḥkhī tyāga-viyogābhyām), one experiences pleasure from abandonment and pain from separation.

The story of the hawk goes like this: A young hawk was once caught by somebody. He made it his pet. He used to feed the hawk regularly with food, etc. When the hawk grew up, he considered releasing it in the forest. The hawk was happy at its release but became afflicted by its separation from its care-taker.

अहिनिर्व्लयिनिवत् ॥ ६ ॥

ahinirvlayinivat ॥ 6 ॥

(ahi-nirvlayini-vat) Just as a snake abandons its old skin [slough]. Similarly, a seeker of mokṣa or self-realisation abandons the material objects after enjoying them for a long time.

छिन्नहस्तवद्वा ॥ ७ ॥

chhinnahastavadvā ॥ 7 ॥

Once the body is abandoned, a self-realised person does not claim it again as a matter of right (chhinnahasta-vadvā), just as the amputated hands cannot be claimed by the person undergoing amputation.

Thus non-possession of material objects helps in self-realisation.

असाधनानुचिन्तनं बन्धाय भरतवत् ॥ ८ ॥

asādhanānuchintanaṁ bandhāya bharatavat ॥ 8 ॥

(anuchintanam) Thinking of (asādhana) the things that are not instrumental to self-realisation (bandhāya) is conducive to bondage (bharatavat) as in the case of Bharata.

The story of Bharata Ṛṣi is as follows: In ancient times, there was a self-realised seer called Bharata. Once, he saw a female deer on the verge of death after giving birth to its young one. He developed a great compassion for the newly born young of the deer and started rearing it. He became so attached to that young one of deer that at the time of death, his mind was fixed upon it. Because of affection for the deer, he did not attain mokṣa but assumed the body of a deer in the next life. The purport of the story is that the deer was not instrumental in self-realisation, so thinking of that and getting attached to it would cause bondage and not liberation.

A yogī should prefer a secluded life rather than a public life. Public life is a hurdle in the way of yoga.

बहुभिर्योगे विरोधोरागादिभिः कुमारीशङ्घवत् ॥ ९ ॥

bahubhiryoge virodho rāgādibhiḥ kumārīśaṅkhavat ॥ 9 ॥

(bahubhir yoge) In public life, due to interaction with others, resulting quarrels and struggles may give rise (rāgādibhiḥ) to passions and aversions (virodhaḥ) which are contrary to yoga (kumārīśaṅkhavat) as jingling is produced by the mutual contact of shell bracelets worn by girls.

द्वाभ्यामपि तथैव ॥ १० ॥

dvābhyāmapi tathaiva ॥ 10 ॥

Even the company of a second person hinders progress in yoga. So, a lonely life in seclusion is best for progress on the path of yoga.

निराशः सुखी पिङ्गलावत ॥ ११ ॥

nirāśaḥ sukhī piṅgalāvata ॥ 11 ॥

He who has (nirāśaḥ) no expectations is (sukhī) happy, (piṅgalāvat) like Piṅgalā, a courtesan, who, desiring a lover, had sleepless nights, but she immediately realised that what she was doing was not good for her, and she should get rid of this hope. When she got over the hope, she had a sound sleep.

Similarly, if a yogī has hopes or expectations, he can never progress on the path of yoga.

अनारम्भेऽपि परगृहे सुखी सर्पवत् ॥ १२ ॥

anārambhe'pi paragṛhe sukhī sarpavat ॥ 12 ॥

A self-realised man is not worried about building his house, āsrama or maṭha. This tendency brings a self-realised person to the level of the common man. There is no difference between a saṁnyāsī or an ordinary man. A self-realised person is happy (anārambhe api) even without his house, (sarpavat) like a serpent finds (sukhī) comfort in having entered the hole made by others [rats]. Similarly, for a yogī, every place is his house.

बहुशास्त्रगुरूपासनेऽपि सारादानं षट्-पदवत् ॥ १३ ॥

bahuśāstragurūpāsane'pi sārādānaṁ ṣaṭpadavat ॥ 13 ॥

It is appreciable (sārādānam) to gather essence from (bahuśāstra-gurūpāsane) the instructions of Gurus and many Śastras for attaining self-realisation (ṣaṭpada-vat) like black bee gathers juices form flowers.

इषुकारवन्नैकचित्तस्य समाधिहानिः ॥ १४ ॥

iṣukāravannaikachittasya samādhihāniḥ ॥ 14 ॥

(naikachittasya) He/she who focuses his/her mind on one object (iṣukārāvat) like a shooter (samādhihāniḥ) does not face interruption in his Samādhi.

कृतनियमलङ्घनादानर्थक्यं लोकवत् ॥ १५ ॥

kṛtaniyamalaṅghanād-ānarthakyaṁ lokavat ॥ 15 ॥

If a seeker (kṛtaniyam-laṅghanāt) violates the rules (yamas, niyamas) made for self-realisation, he (ānarthakyam) will fail in his aim of self-realisation (lokavat) as in ordinary life, a person violating the regulations of health fails in maintaining health.

तद्विस्मरणेऽपि भेकीवत् ॥ १६ ॥

tadvismaraṇe'pi bhekīvat ॥ 16 ॥

(tadvismaraṇe api) If a seeker forgets the rules and regulations set for self-realisation, he will also face failure (bhekīvat), like the king failed to regain his wife in the story of a female frog.

The story goes like this: Once upon a time, a king set out for hunting. In the forest, he came across a beautiful girl. He inquired about her and proposed to marry her. She became ready to marry the king on the condition that whenever the king showed her water, she would disappear. But, on one occasion, fatigued by sport, she asked the king for water. King, too, forgetting the condition, presented water to her. She then assumes the form of a female frog and disappears after seeing the water. King tried hard to search for her, but all was in vain. The purport of the story is that a seeker on the path of spirituality never achieves success if he starts forgetting rules and regulations.

Self-realisation can be attained through śravaṇa [hearing], manana [thinking] and nididhyāsana [constant brooding over what has been heard and thought of]. Emphasis on the same has been laid down in the next sūtra:

नोपदेशश्रवणेऽपि कृतकृत्यता.परामर्शादृतेविरोचनवत् ॥ १७ ॥

nopadeśaśravaṇe'pi kṛtakṛtyatā parāmarśādṛte virochanavat ॥17

(api) Merely (upadeśa śravaṇe) hearing of instructions is (kṛtakṛtyatā) not going to help in self-realisation (ṛte) until and unless there are (prāmarśāt) proper deliberations in the form of manana [thinking] and nididhyāsana [brooding over] what has been heard from Guru, (virochanavat) like Virochana who could not attain self-realisation even after hearing the instructions for it from Prajāpati. In contrast, Indra, his classmate, succeeded, as he subjected the instructions to deliberations.

दृष्टस्तयोरिन्द्रस्य ॥ १८ ॥

dṛṣṭastayorindrasya ॥ 18 ॥

(tayoḥ) Of the two, [Virochana and Indra], (indrasya dṛṣṭaḥ) Indra is seen to have attained self-realisation.

प्रणतिब्रह्मचर्योपसर्पणानि कृत्वा सिद्धिर्बहुकालात् तद्वत् ॥ १९॥

praṇatibrahmacharyopasarpaṇāni kṛtvā siddhir bahukālāt
tadvat ।। 19

(praṇati) Thus, having paid respect to Guru, (brahmacharya) observed Brahmacharya [meditation upon Brahman] and (upasarpaṇāvi) resided close to Guru, one (siddhiḥ) succeeds in self-realisation (bahukālāt) after a long practice of time, (tadvat) like Indra.

How much time does self-realisation take? To this, the author replies:

न कालनियमो वामदेववत् ॥ २० ॥

na kālaniyamo vāmadevavat ॥ 20 ॥

(na kāla niyamaḥ) There is no particular limit of time. As soon as a seeker gets his/her sanskāras of the external world eliminated and identifies his/her true nature, he attains self-realisation. This may happen very late or immediately, (vāmadeva-vat) like Vāmadeva, who had self-realisation in the womb of his mother due to the absence of all past-life sanskāras and identification of his true nature.

Through meditation upon the nature of ātman, as described in the tradition of self-realised Gurus, one can attain self-realisation. The same is described in the next sūtra.

अध्यस्तरूपोपासनात् पारम्पर्येण यज्ञोपासकानामिव ॥ २१ ॥

Adhyastarūpopāsanāt pāramparyeṇa yajñopāsakānāmiva ॥ 21 ॥

(upāsanāt) Suppose we meditate upon (adhyastarūpa) the nature of ātman (pāramparyeṇa) as described in Guru tradition. In that case, we can have the benefit of self-realisation, as a performer of yajña gets the benefits of performance of yajña like purification of the environment, induction of rain, and others.

Here, one may raise a question that Pañchāgni yajña has been appreciated in the Upaniṣads. If a seeker does pañchāgni yajña [basking in the sun in June by burning fire in four directions], does he/she need to follow the means to self-realisation? The answer is:

इतरलाभेऽप्यावृत्तिः पञ्चाग्नियोगतो जन्मश्रुतेः ॥ २२ ॥

itaralābhe'pyāvṛttiḥ pañchāgniyogato janmaśruteḥ ॥ 22 ॥

(itaralābhe api) Although there are many other benefits (pañchāgniyogataḥ) of pañchāgni yajña, like tolerance to heat and cold, but they are not helpful in self-realisation. Practitioners of pañchāgni yajña are also (janmaśruteḥ) heard to undergo the cycle of birth and death.

Only an ascetic [renunciate] can attain self-realisation. This is emphasised in the next sūtra.

विरक्तस्य हेयहानमुपादेयोपादानं हंसक्षीरवत् ॥ २३ ॥

viraktasya heyahānamupādeyopādānaṁ haṁsakṣīravat ॥ 23 ॥

(viraktasya) Only an ascetic (heya-hānam) can abandon what is worth abandoning and (upādeya-upādānam) attain what is worth attaining (hansa-kṣīravat) as a swan alone can take milk when water and milk are mixed together.

Now, the question arises as to why only an ascetic can attain self-realisation and not others. The answer is as follows:

लब्धातिशाययोगाद्वा तद्वत् ॥ २४ ॥

labdhātiśayayogādvā tadvat ॥ 24 ॥

An ascetic can attain self-realisation (labdhātiśaya-yogāt vā) because of the powers gained through yoga [samādhi]. (tadvat) Just as a swan has the capability to separate milk from water, other birds are not endowed with such a capability.

Some do's and don'ts are also prescribed for the

seeker of self-realisation. For example,

न कामचारित्वं रागोपहते शुकवत् ॥ २५ ॥

na kāmachāritvaṁ rāgopahate śukavat ॥ 25 ॥

The seeker of self-realisation (kāmachāritvam) should avoid the company of those (rāgopahate) attached to sensory objects, as a parrot makes the distance from people for fear of being captured by them.

Why is the company of persons attached to sensory objects harmful? The same is explained further with an example.

गुणयोगाद्बद्धः शुकवत् ॥ २६ ॥

guṇayogādbaddhaḥ śukavat ॥ 26 ॥

Should a seeker keep the company of persons attached to sensory objects (guṇayogāt baddhaḥ), on account of their company, he also develops an attachment to sensory objects, resulting in his bondage (śukavat) as a parrot incurs bondage on account of the rope of the hunter.

न भोगाद्रागशान्तिर्मुनिवत् ॥ २७ ॥

na bhogādrāgaśāntirmunivat ॥ 27 ॥

(bhogāt) Because the bhoga [enjoyment] of sensory objects will (na) not help a seeker (rāgaśāntih) control his desire for sensory objects, as in the case of a sage called Saubhari. He tried to satisfy his desire for bhoga of sensory objects for years together but never got satisfied; ultimately, he declared -

आमृत्युतो नैव मनोरथानामन्तोऽस्ति विज्ञातं मयाद्य ।
मनोरथासक्तिपरस्य चित्तं न जायते वै परमार्थसंगि ॥

āmṛtyuto naiva manorathānāmanto'sti vijñātaṁ mayādya ।

*manorathāsaktiparasya   chittaṁ   na   jāyate   vai
paramārthasaṁgi* ।।

[Meaning] Today, I am convinced that desires for the bhoga of sensory objects will not be satisfied till death, and a person indulged in the bhoga of sensory objects can never attain the highest objective of one's life [self-realisation].

How can one develop vairāgya [renunciation]? To this reply is given as follows:

दोषदर्शनादुभयोः ॥ २८ ॥

doṣadarśanādubhayoḥ ॥ 28 ॥

(doṣa-darśanāt ubhayoḥ) In realising the problems of both, i.e. in the bondage of soul and indulgence in the bhoga [enjoyment] of sensory objects, one develops vairāgya [renunciation or ascetism].

Note: Problem in bondage of the soul and bhoga is pain and suffering.

न मलिनचेतस्युपदेशबीजप्ररोहोऽजवत् ॥ २९ ॥

na malinachetasyupadeśa bījapraroho'javat ॥ 29 ॥

(upadeśa bīja prarohaḥ) The seed of instructions does not grow (Malina-chetasi) in the mind corrupted by the desire for bhoga, such as a king named Aja could not be soothed by the instructions of Ṛṣi Vasiṣṭha whose mind was disturbed by the grief at the death of his beloved wife.

नाभासमात्रमपि मलिनदर्पणवत् ॥ ३० ॥

nābhāsamātramapi malinadarpaṇavat ॥ 30 ॥

The mind corrupted by rāga and dveṣa (na ābhāsa-mātram) does not have a tinge of reflection of self-realisation (malina-darpana-vat) as the defective mirror does reflect an object.

न तज्जस्यापि तद्रूपता पङ्कजवत् ॥ ३१ ॥

na tajjasyāpi tadrūpatā paṅkajavat ॥ 31 ॥

(tajjasyāpi) Although self-realisation is produced with the help of Prakṛti, (na tadrūpatā) the experience of the soul in the state of self-realisation is not the same as when in bondage [without self-realisation]. (paṅkaja-vat) This is like a lotus grown in the mud but inherits no quality of mud.

न भूतियोगेऽपिकृतकृत्यतोपास्यसिद्धिवदुपास्यसिद्धिवत् ॥ ३२ ॥

na bhūtiyoge'pi kṛtakṛtyatopāsyasiddhivadupāsyasiddhivat ॥32

(bhūtiyoge) Vibhūti yoga [divine powers attained as the reward of yoga] is (api) also (na) not going to help (kṛtakṛtyatā) in self-realisation, as all these divine powers are shortlived and a hindrance to self-realisation, (upāsyasiddhi-vat) as the happiness gained through the achievement of the desired goal or object is short-lived [provides momentary happiness, not permanent].

Fifth Chapter

In the first three chapters, the fundamental tenets of Sāṅkhya have been described. In the fourth chapter, the same principles were supported by some practical examples and popular stories prevalent in society. In the fifth chapter, certain other such issues related or unrelated to self-realisation will be examined, as can stand contrary to the fundamental principles of Sāṅkhya.

According to Sāṅkhya, discrimination between Soul and body leads to apavarga [self-realisation]. Here, a question can be raised: if discrimination between soul and body leads to self-realisation, then what is the need to do sāttvika actions prescribed in Vedas and Śāstras? To this, the author replies:

मङ्गलाचरणं शिष्टाचारात्फलदर्शनच्छुतितश्चेति ॥ १ ॥

maṅgalācharaṇaṁ śiṣṭāchārātphaladarśanāchchhutitaścheti ‖ *1* ‖

(maṅgalācharaṇam) The performance of good actions/karmas is not just recommended, it is a necessity, (śiṣṭāchārāt) as the conduct of high-profile seers and saints unequivocally supports this. Furthermore, (phaladarśanam) we can see that no fruit can be reaped without action, so good/sāttvika action conducive to mokṣa is indispensable. (śrutitaścha) This has also been confirmed by Vedic texts.

"कुर्वन्नेवेह कर्माणि" Yajurveda (40.1)

"kurvanneveha karmāṇi"

[Meaning] Doing good actions, one can desire to live for a hundred years.

"देवो वः सविता प्रार्पयतु श्रेष्ठतमाय कर्मणे" Yajurveda (1.1) *"devo vaḥ savitā prārpayatu śreṣṭhatamāya karmaṇe"*

[Meaning] Let the Savitā [Creator Brahman and creator of life on earth, the sun] lead you to perform good actions.

Hereunder, the author quotes some possible doubts about the governorship of Iśvara raised during those days.

नेश्वराधिष्ठिते फलनिष्पत्तिः कर्मणा तत्सिद्धेः ॥२॥

neśvarādhiṣṭhite phalaniṣpattiḥ karmaṇā tatsiddheḥ ॥2॥

(Īśvarādhiṣṭhite) Under the intervention of the governorship of Iśvara [Brahman], (na) it is not possible (phalaniṣpattiḥ) to get the fruits in conformity with the karmas. Getting fruits in conformity with the karmas will only be possible if there is no intervention of Iśvara and (tatsiddheḥ) fruits are produced (karmaṇā) by karmas themselves.

स्वोपकारादधिष्ठानं लोकवत् ॥ ३ ॥

svopakārādadhiṣṭhānaṁ lokavat ॥ 3 ॥

(adhiṣṭhānam) Suppose Iśvara is admitted as the governor of the universe. (svopakārāt) In that case, he may act for His own benefit like (lokavat) other ordinary human beings in the world.

लौकिकेश्वरवदितरथा ॥ ४ ॥

laukikeśvaravaditarathā ॥ 4 ॥

(itarathā) If we say that Iśvara never intends for his own benefit, but He always intends for the benefit of souls, in that case, (laukikeśvaravat) He will be placed in the category of other governors [rulers] in the world who intend for the wellbeing of their nationals.

In all three cases, the governorship of Īśvara is not tenable. So, He should be viewed in some other role.

पारिभाषिको वा ॥ ५ ॥

paribhāṣiko vā ॥ 5 ॥

Thus, if we remove Īśvara from the role of governorship because he cannot intend either for His own benefit or for the benefit of souls, as either way, intending makes Īśvara endowed with rāga (attachment), and rāga is the qualification of an ordinary human being in the world. At this stage, his existence would be meaningless (pāribhāṣiko vā); he will be there for the namesake or the subject of the dictionary.

न रागाद्दते तत्सिद्धि: प्रतिनियतकारणत्वात् ॥ ६ ॥

na rāgādṛte tatsiddhi: pratiniyatakāraṇatvāt ॥ 6 ॥

(na rāgāt ṛte) Without rāga [attachment], (tatsiddhiḥ) Īśvara cannot intend to create the world (pratiniyata) because rāga is a fixed or singular cause of any tendency.

तद्योगेऽपि न नित्यमुक्त: ॥ ७ ॥

tadyoge'pi na nityamuktaḥ ॥ 7 ॥

(tadyoge) If Īśvara creates the world with the help of Prakṛti, He (na) cannot be called (nityamuktaḥ) eternally liberated, as for the period of creation, He will be known in bondage.

प्रधानशक्तियोगाच्चेत्सङ्गापत्ति: ॥ ८ ॥

pradhānaśaktiyogāchchetsaṅgāpattiḥ ॥ 8 ॥

Moreover, (chet) should you say that creative power is vested with Prakṛti being the material cause and Īśvara is said to have creative power or the material cause of creation (pradhāna-śakti-yogāt) because of the proximity or conjunction with Prakṛti. In this case, (saṅgāpattiḥ) He will be blamed for seeking the help of the others.

One can say that there is no need for Prakṛti in the creation of the world; Iśvara may be accepted to have created the whole world singularly with his own power. The answer is:

सत्तामात्राच्चेत्सर्वैश्वर्यम् ॥ ९ ॥

sattāmātrāchchetsarvaiśvaryam ॥ *9* ॥

If Iśvara is the material cause of creation (sattāmātrāt) on His own or account of His mere existence, then the whole world will be the effect [product] of Iśvara.

प्रमाणाभावान्न तत्सिद्धिः ॥ १० ॥

pramāṇābhāvānna tatsiddhiḥ ॥ *10* ॥

Moreover, (pramāṇabhāvat) there is no proof that (na tatsiddhiḥ) Iśvara subjects to change because the material cause undergoes change when something is caused by it.

संबन्धाभावान्नानुमानम् ॥११॥

sambandhābhāvānnānumānam ॥*11*॥

Also, (sambandhābhāvāt) because of the lack of such practical examples as prove that insentient matter can be created from sentient [chetana] entity, (anumānam na) we cannot infer that the material world is created from immaterial [chetana] Iśvara.

Note: We have practical examples of ornaments made of gold and pots made of mud; such examples prove that material things are created from their material cause.

श्रुतिरपि प्रधानकार्यत्वस्य ॥ १२ ॥

śrutirapi pradhānakāryatvasya ॥ *12* ॥

(śrutiḥ api) Vedas also describe this creation as the (pradhānakāryatvasya) effect of material cause, Prakṛti.

नाविद्याशक्तियोगो निःसङ्गस्य ॥ १३ ॥

nāvidyāśaktiyogo niḥsaṅgasya ॥ *13* ॥

All-knowing Īśvara, (nisaṅgasya) who is independent, (na) cannot have (yogaḥ) contact with (avidyā-śakti) Prakṛti endowed with the power of avidyā [mistaken identity].

Note: The soul is not all-knowing, so it can identify itself with Prakṛti and connect with it [become embodied].

तद्योगे तत्सिद्धावन्योन्याश्रयत्वम् ॥ १४ ॥

tadyoge tatsiddhāvanyonyāśrayatvam ॥ *14* ॥

(tatsiddhau) The connection of Prakṛti (body) with the soul takes place (tadyoge) on account of the conjunction of the soul with avidyā [identifying itself with Prakṛti [body]. Thus, the connection of avidyā with the soul and the connection of the soul with Prakṛti [body] are interdependent.

This may lead to a debate about whether the connection of the body with the soul occurs first or the connection of avidyā with the soul occurs first, as without the connection of avidya with the soul, the connection of the soul with the body is not possible. When the connection of the soul with the body occurs, we learn about the connection of avidyā with the soul. This would lead to the unending debate about seed and sprout, as to whether the seed came first or the sprout. To this, the author replies:

न बीजाङ्कुरवत्सादिसंसारश्रुतेः ॥ १५ ॥

na bījāṅkuravatsādisaṃsāraśruteḥ ॥ 15 ॥

(na) It is not (bījāñkuravat) like the case of seed and sprout. The circle of seed and sprout is beginningless. The Vedic texts teach that the mundane life of the soul [embodiment of the soul or connection of the soul with the Prakṛti] has a beginning. It is not beginningless like seed and sprout.

Vidyā means identifying the true nature of something. Avidyā means identifying something for something else. Suppose you do not accept this definition of avidyā and maintain that avidyā is different from vidyā and is eternal and unchangeable. Brahman, connecting with this avidyā, becomes the material cause of creation. The answer is given below:

विद्यातोऽन्यत्वेब्रह्मबाधप्रसङ्गः ॥ १६ ॥

vidyāto'nyatve brahmabādhaprasaṅgaḥ ॥ 16 ॥

(vidyātaḥ) Had avidyā been (anyatve) a different permanent entity from vidyā, and in its association, Brahman became the material cause of the creation. (brahma-bādha-prasaṅgaḥ) Avidyā would abolish the existence of Brahman, as the same may replace Brahman.

अबाधे नैष्फल्यम् ॥ १७ ॥

abādhe naiṣphalyam ॥ 17 ॥

If you say that even in this situation, (abādhe) avidyā is not going to abolish the existence of Brahman, then (naiṣphalyam) the existence of 'Avidyā' becomes useless.

विद्याबाध्यत्वे जगतोऽप्येवम् ॥ १८ ॥

vidyābādhyatve jagato'pyevam ॥ *18* ॥

(vidyā) Vidyā (bādhyatve) abolishes Avidyā. Should you say that this visible world is of the nature of avidyā, (jagataḥ) then it would (api evam) also be abolished by vidyā for the self-realised person. But, in reality, it does not happen. It proves that this visible world is not of the form of Avidyā or the effect [product] of Avidyā.

If we insist that avidyā is of the form of Jagat [visible world], then avidyā will not be abolished by vidyā, like the Jagat.

तद्रूपत्वे सादित्वम् ॥ १९ ॥

tadrūpatve sāditvam ॥ *19* ॥

(tadrūpatve) If avidyā were of the nature of Jagat [visible world], (sādi-tvam) it would also have its beginning like Jagat. Then avidyā cannot be considered anādi or eternal and cannot be associated with the eternal Brahman.

न धर्मापलापः प्रकृतिकार्यवैचित्र्यात् ॥ २० ॥

na dharmāpalāpaḥ Prakṛtikāryavaichitrayāt ॥ *20* ॥

(Prakṛtikārya-vaichitryāt) The diversity of the bodies and other products of Prakṛti [matter] is caused by the permutation and combination of sattva, rajas and tamas guṇas of Prakṛti. (na dharmāpalāpaḥ) Still, in this diversity, the contribution of dhārmika [moral and ethical] or adhārmika [immoral and unethical] karmas done by embodied souls cannot be ruled out.

NB: Here, the author wants to say that the diversity in the bodies or other products of Prakṛti [matter] is not only due to the permutation and combination of sattva, rajas, and tamas guṇas of Prakṛti, but it is also due to the kārmika sanskāras of embodied souls, as various souls are required to reap different fruits according to their different dhārmika and adhārmika karmas.

श्रुतिलिङ्गादिभिस्तत्सिद्धिः ॥ २१ ॥

śrutiliṅgādibhistatsiddhiḥ ॥ 21 ॥

(tatsiddhiḥ) The contribution of dhārmika and adhārmika karmas to the diversity of bodies and products of matter is established by (śruti) the authority of Vedic texts, (liṅga) inference, (ādibhiḥ) and perception of yogīs in Samādhi.

Hereunder, we illustrate the above facts with examples.

Vedic Texts:

The Ṛgveda (10.81.3) says:

विश्वतंश्चक्षुरुत विश्वतोंमुखो विश्वतोंबाहुरुत विश्वतंस्पात् ।

सं बाहुभ्यां धर्मति सं पतंत्रैर्द्यावाभूमीं जनयंन्देव एकं: ॥

viśvataścakṣuruta viśvatomukho viśvatobāhuruta viśvataspāt, sam bāhubhyāṃ dhamati sam patatrairdyāvābhūmī janayandeva ekaḥ.

[Meaning] The sole self-refulgent maker created stars and planets accommodating bodies of souls with diverse eyes, organs of speech, hands and legs. The embodied souls attain these bodies (bāhubhyām) because of their dhārmika and adhārmika karmas, like birds, reach their destinations because of their wings.

Bṛhadāraṇyaka Upaniṣad (4.4.5) says:

पुण्यः पुण्येन कर्मणा भवति पापः पापेन ।

puṇyaḥ puṇyena karmaṇā bhavati pāpaḥ pāpena,

[Meaning] A soul attains lower species by dint of its lower karmas and good bodies by dint of its good karmas.

Inference:

Seeing the 84 lakh species, one can infer that these diverse bodies are created to accommodate souls with various dhārmika and adhārmika karmas.

Yogīs Perception:

Yogīs know from Samādhi that various diverse material bodies are created to accommodate souls with various dhārmika [righteous] and adhārmika [unrighteous] karmas.

But in the next sūtra, the author says that the role of karmas in the diversity of bodies and products of matter should not be perceived as a thumb rule, as there are other factors like permutation and combination of sattva, rajas and tamas.

न नियमः प्रमाणान्तरावकाशात् ॥ २२ ॥

na niyamaḥ pramāṇāntarāvakāśāt ॥ 22 ॥

(na niyamaḥ) The contribution of dhārmika and adhārmika karmas to the diversity of bodies and products of matter is not taken as exclusive (pramāṇāntarāvakāśāt) factor as other factors like permutation and combination of sattva, rajas and tamas, the guṇas of Prakṛti also play their part.

उभयत्राप्येवम् ॥ २३ ॥

ubhayatrāpyevam ॥ *23* ॥

(evam) The above factors contribute to diversity (ubhayatra) here [in present life] and hereafter [future life].

अर्थात्सिद्धिश्चेत्समानमुभयोः ॥ २४ ॥

arthātsiddhiśchetsamānamubhayoḥ ॥ *24* ॥

(chet) If (arthāt) the role [purpose] of any one factor in diverse creation is (siddhiḥ) established, (samānam Ubhayoḥ) the role of both factors is equally deemed established.

अन्तःकरणधर्मत्वं धर्मादीनाम् ॥ २५ ॥

antaḥkaraṇadharmatvaṁ dharmādīnām ॥ *25* ॥

(dharmādīnām) Sanskāras of dharma and adharma born of sattva, rajas and tamas are the (antaḥkaraṇadharmatvam) property of mind, not soul, as they are made of Prakṛti and mind is also made of Prakṛti. However, they are experienced by the soul. They also exist in the mind even during pralaya [dissolution].

गुणादीनां च नात्यन्तबाधः ॥ २६ ॥

guṇādīnāṁ cha nātyantabādhaḥ ॥ *26* ॥

(guṇādīnāṁ) In this case, when sanskāras of dharma and adharma are accepted as the property of the mind, the utility of guṇas in the bhoga and apavarga of the soul (na atyantabādhaḥ) cannot be completely ruled out.

If the pain and pleasure are not the properties of the soul, how does the soul experience them?

पञ्चावयवयोगात्सुखसंवित्तिः ॥ २७ ॥

panchāvayavayogātsukhasaṁvittiḥ ॥ 27 ॥

(sukha-saṁvittiḥ) The soul experiences pain or pleasure (pañchāvayava-yogāt) through the five sense organs.

Sūtra no. 21 says that the contribution of dhārmika and adhārmika karmas to the diversity of bodies and products of matter is proved by inference. In the next sūtra, the nature of inference is explained.

न सकृद्ग्रहणात्संबन्धसिद्धिः ॥ २८ ॥

na sakṛdgrahaṇātsambandhasiddhiḥ ॥ 28 ॥

(sakṛt grahaṇāt) If two things are once spotted together, (sambandha-siddhiḥ) that does not establish a permanent connection between them.

If an elephant is spotted close to fire, that does not mean there will be elephants where there is fire.

Note: Permanent connection is called vyāpti [pervadedness] in technical terms of Sāṅkhya.

Nature of vyāpti is explained in the next sūtra:

नियतधर्म साहित्यमुभयो रेकतरस्य वा व्याप्तिः ॥ २९ ॥

niyatadharma sāhityamubhayo rekatarasya vā vyāptiḥ ॥ 29 ॥

(vyāptiḥ) Vyāpti [pervadedness] is (niyat-dharma sāhityam) the permanent mutual association (ubhayoḥ) of two dharmas or things (vā) or the (ekatarasya) association of either of them to the other.

For example, smoke is permanently associated with fire, but fire is not permanently associated with smoke. As such, where there is smoke, there will be fire, but where there is fire, there doesn't need to be smoke.

न तत्त्वान्तरं वस्तुकल्पनाप्रसक्तेः ॥ ३० ॥

na tattvāntaram vastukalpanāprasakteḥ ॥ 30 ॥

This Vyāpti [pervadedness] or permanent connection between two objects (na) is not (tattvāntaram) an entity other than the 25 entities of Sāṅkhya, for it is unsuitable to postulate a permanent connection as an entity.

निजशक्त्युद्भवमित्याचार्याः ॥ ३१ ॥

nijaśaktyudbhavamityāchāryāḥ ॥ 31 ॥

(ti-āchāryaḥ) But certain Āchāryas say that vyāpti [pervadedness] is (nijaśakti-bhavan) the manifestation of the innate power of objects having a permanent connection in the form of cause or effect.

आधेयशक्तियोग इति पञ्चशिखः ॥ ३२ ॥

ādheyaśaktiyoga iti pañchaśikhaḥ ॥ 32 ॥

(iti Pañchaśikhaḥ) According to Āchārya Pañchaśikha, (yogaḥ) pervadedness or vyāpti [the connection between pervader [ādhāra or vyāpaka] and pervaded [ādheya or vyāpya] takes place (ādheyaśakti) due to the power of being the effect [product] of pervaded. For instance, fire is ādhāra or vyāpaka [pervader], and smoke is ādheya or vyāpya [pervaded]. So, the connection of fire with smoke takes place due to the power of the smoke being the product of fire.

Note: Here, the smoke and fire are connected with each other as effect and cause.

न स्वरूपशक्तिर्नियमः पुनर्वादिप्रसक्तेः ॥ ३३ ॥

na svarūpaśaktirniyamaḥ punarvādaprasakteḥ ॥ 33 ॥

We cannot say that the power of connection [effect] of pervaded [smoke] with pervader [fire] is not different from the essential nature [effect] of pervaded [smoke]. This will be a mere repetition of the same thing.

If we say smoke has the power to connect with fire, being its effect or that the essential nature of smoke is to connect with fire, it is one and the same thing or a mere repetition of the same concept.

विशेषणानर्थक्यप्रसक्तेः ॥ ३४ ॥

viśeṣaṇānarthakyaprasakteḥ ॥ 34 ॥

(viśeṣaṇa-ānarthakya-prasakteḥ) Moreover, if smoke has the nature of vyāpti or pervadedness, it is useless to use the word pervadedness as the adjective for smoke. It will be like repeating the same name, 'Ravi Ravi'. Here, it is useless to apply 'Ravi' as an adjective of 'Ravi'.

पल्लवादिष्वनुपपत्तेश्च ॥ ३५ ॥

pallavādiṣvanupapatteścha ॥ 35 ॥

Further, the argument that the power of pervadedness is the essential nature of pervaded [smoke] (pallavādiṣu anupapatteścha) does not hold universally true in the case of leaves and others. For instance, the power of pervadedness in leaves [pervaded] is not their essential nature because when a leave falls or is cut off the tree, its essential nature [of pervadedness] is also eliminated since it no longer remains the means of inference of the tree existing at a particular place.

आधेयशक्तिसिद्धौ निजशक्तियोगः समानन्यायात् ॥ ३६ ॥

ādheyaśaktisiddhau nijaśaktiyogaḥ samānanyāyāt ॥ 36 ॥

(ādheyaśaktau) Were it settled that a particular thing

has the power of pervadedness, (samāna-nyāyāt) on the same pattern, (nijaśakti-yogaḥ) it may also be known that pervadedness is the essential nature of that very thing.

Explaining the nature of vyāpti as one of the main factors in anumāna [inference] leading to the knowledge of invisible entities, in the next sūtra, the author will explain śabda-pramāṇa [word as the means of cognition].

वाच्यवाचकभावः संबन्धःशब्दार्थयोः ॥ ३७ ॥

vāchyavāchakabhāvaḥ sambandhaḥ śabdārthayoḥ ॥ 37 ॥

(śabdārthayoḥ) The word and the object signified by it (sambandhaḥ) are related to each other as (vāchaka) signifying and (vāchya) signified.

त्रिभिः संबन्धसिद्धिः ॥ ३८ ॥

tribhiḥ sambandhasiddhiḥ ॥ 38 ॥

(sambandha-siddhiḥ) The relation between word and the object signified by it is established by (tribhiḥ) three means.

The three means are:

1. Āptopadeśa: Instructions by a seer or enlightened yogī. Vedic texts and six Darśanas are included in the category of Āptopadeśa.

2. Vṛddha-vyavahāra: Practice by an expert. Whatever a student learns from the teacher is contained in the category of Vṛddha-vyavahāra.

3. Prasiddha-pada-samānādhikaraṇya or Prasiddha-pada-sānnidhya: To know the unknown object signified by some word together with the known objects or actions denoted by the other word. As a child that already knows the mango tree and spring season signified

by some words, when it hears the word, 'In Spring season, cuckoo chirps on mango tree,' then understands the bird 'cuckoo' also when it chirps in spring on mango tree.

न कार्ये नियम उभयथा दर्शनात् ॥ ३९ ॥

na kārye niyama ubhayathā darśanāt ॥ 39 ॥

The relation of signifying and signified (na kārye niyamaḥ) not only exists between verbs and actions signified by verbs, (ubhayathā darśanat) but also seen between words and objects signified by words.

लोके व्युत्पन्नस्य वेदार्थप्रतीतिः ॥ ४० ॥

loke vyutpannasya vedārthapratītiḥ ॥ 40 ॥

(loke vyutpannasya) He who is accomplished in knowing the significance of laukika words (vedārtha-pratītiḥ) understands the intended sense of the Veda.

There is a saying,

य एव लौकिकास्त एव वैदिकाः शब्दाः ।

ya ēva laukikāsta ēva vaidikāḥ śabdāḥ

[Meaning] There is no difference between Vedic and laukika words.

न त्रिभिरपौरुषेयत्वाद्वेदस्य तदर्थस्यातीन्द्रियत्वात् ॥ ४१ ॥

na tribhirapauruṣeyatvādvedasya tadarthasyātīndriyatvāt ॥ 41

Since (vedasya apauṣeyatvāt) the knowledge of the Veda pertains to Brahman and its meaning (tadarthasya atīndriyatvāt) is beyond the reach of sensory perception, (na) so it cannot be congnised (tribhiḥ) by three means of establishing relation between word and object, as described in sūtra 38 above.

To this, the author replies:

न यज्ञादेः स्वरूपतो धर्मत्वं वैशिष्ट्यात् ॥ ४२ ॥

na yajñādeḥ svarūpato dharmatvaṁ vaiśiṣṭyāt ॥ 42 ॥

(na) It is incorrect to say that Vedas signify something beyond the reach of sensory perception (yajñādeḥ) as the process of creation and its knowledge is (vaiśiṣṭyāt) specifically (svarūpataḥ dharmatvam) the subject matter of the Veda. And this creation and its knowledge are not beyond the reach of our sensory perception.

निजशक्तिर्व्युत्पत्त्या व्यवच्छिद्यते ॥ ४३ ॥

nijaśaktirvyutpattyā vyavachchhidyate ॥ 43 ॥

The Veda is Apauruṣeya [information or knowledge in Brahman], yet the (nijaśaktiḥ) intended sense of its words (vyavachchhidyate) is ascertained (vyutpattyā) through the etymology by the seers at the beginning of creation and transmitted to us in succession.

योग्यायोग्येषु प्रतीतिजनकत्वात्तत्सिद्धिः ॥ ४४ ॥

yogyāyogyeṣu pratītijanakatvāttatsiddhiḥ ॥ 44 ॥

(yogyāyogyeṣu) Just as the objects subjected to sensory perception (pratītijanakatvāt) are understood by the three means, similarly, the objects that are beyond the reach of sensory perception (tatsiddhiḥ) can be understood by three means— 1. Āptopadeśa [Instructions by a seer or enlightened yogī], 2. Vṛddha-vyavahāra [Practice by an expert], 3. Prasiddha-pada-sānnidhya [to know the unknown object together with the known object] is described in sūtra 38 above.

न नित्यत्वं वेदानां कार्यत्वश्रुतेः ॥ ४५ ॥

na nityatvaṁ vedānāṁ kāryatvaśruteḥ ॥ 45 ॥

(vedānāṁ nityatvaṁ na) Vedas [knowledge of Brahman reflected through creation] are not eternal, (śruteḥ) as Vedic texts describe them (kāryatvaṁ) as produced [reflected] through the yajña [process of creation]. For instance, the *Śatapatha Brāhmaṇa* (11.5.8.3) says:

तस्माद् यज्ञात्सर्वहुतः ऋचः सामानि जज्ञिरे ।
छन्दाᳵसि जज्ञिरे तस्माद् यजुस्तस्मादजायत ॥

tasmād yajñātsarvahutaḥ ṛcaḥ sāmāni jajñire.
chandāṁsi jajñire tasmād yajus-tasmādajāyata

[Meaning] Through the Yajña (the process of creation), in which oblations of sattva, rajas and tamas guṇas were made, originated Ṛchas, Sāmans, Yajuṣas and other Chhandas [Atharvaveda].

Thus, knowledge of creation exists in Brahman eternally, but for people like us, it comes into existence after the creation. So, knowledge of creation that comes into being after creation is not eternal.

न पौरुषेयत्वं तत्कर्तुः पुरुषस्याभावात् ॥ ४६ ॥

na pauruṣeyatvaṁ tatkartuḥ puruṣasyābhāvāt ॥ 46 ॥

(pauruṣeyatvaṁ na) The Vedas are not the work of a human being (puruṣasya abhāvāt) because no human being composed them.

मुक्तामुक्तयोरयोग्यत्वात् ॥ ४७ ॥

muktāmuktayorayogyatvāt ॥ 47 ॥

(muktāmuktayoḥ) Both liberated and non-liberated human beings (ayogyatvāt) are not capable of composing the Vedas.

If we say that Vedas are Apauruṣeyas [not composed by human beings], i.e. knowledge of Brahman, then we must consider them eternal. To this, the seer replies.

नापौरुषेयत्वान्नित्यत्वमङ्कुरादिवत् ॥ ४८ ॥

nāpauruṣeyatvānnityatvamaṅkurādivat ॥ *48* ॥

(apauruṣeyāt) If something is not the work of human being [i.e. the work of Brahman], (na nityatvam) that is not the proof of its eternity, as in the case of sprouts and others. Sprouts are not the work of human beings, and they are still not eternal.

तेषामपि तद्योगे दृष्टबाधादिप्रसक्तिः ॥ ४९ ॥

teṣāmapi tadyoge dṛṣṭabādhādiprasaktiḥ ॥ *49* ॥

(teṣām api tadyoge) If we assume that sprouts are the work of human beings like pots and others, (dṛṣṭabādhā-ādi-prasakti) then we shall have to face the problem of proving the maker of sprouts [or making the maker of sprouts visible) and imagine an invisible maker, which is again the Brahman.

Then, what is the nature of objects made by human beings?

यस्मिन्नदृष्टेऽपि कृतबुद्धिरुपजायते तत्पौरुषेयम् ॥ ५० ॥

yasminnadṛṣṭe'pi kṛtabuddhirupajāyate tatpauruṣeyam ॥ *50* ॥

(tat-pauruṣeyatvam) The work of a human being is that (kṛt-buddhir upajāyate) which gives one a notion of its being produced or composed by some human being, (yasmin-adṛṣe'pi) even without seeing it.

निजशक्त्यभिव्यक्तेःस्वतः प्रामाण्यम् ॥ ५१ ॥

nijaśaktyabhivyakteḥ svataḥ prāmāṇyam ॥ *51* ॥

(nija-śakti-abhivyakteḥ) Vedas are the expression of Brahman's own power of creation, so they are self-authority.

The nature of non-entity is explained hereunder.

नासतः ख्यानं नृश्रृङ्गवत् ॥ ५२ ॥

nāsataḥ khyānam nṛśṛṅgavat ॥ 52 ॥

(asataḥ) A non-entity (na) can't (khyānam) be cognised, (nṛśṛṅgavat) like the horn of man.

The nature of the entity is also explained hereunder.

न सतो बाधदर्शनात् ॥ ५३ ॥

na sato bādhadarśanāt ॥ 53 ॥

(bādha) The absence of (sataḥ) an entity is (na) (darśanāt) not seen.

The nature of anirvachanīya (which cannot be described as entity or no-entity) is explained hereunder.

नानिर्वचनीयस्य तदभावात् ॥ ५४ ॥

nānirvachanīyasya tadabhāvāt ॥ 54 ॥

(anirvachanīyasya) Cognisance of an indescribable thing is (na) not possible (tadabhāvāt) because such a thing does not exist. Both things cannot exist simultaneously. For example, both wave and particle conditions cannot exist simultaneously. Either it will be a wave or particle at one time.

About the question of possibility of cognisance of something into other, the reply is as under:

नान्यथाख्यातिः स्ववचोव्याघातात् ॥ ५५ ॥

nānyathākhyātiḥ svavachovyāghātāt ॥ 55 ॥

(na anyathā-khyātiḥ) Neither the cognisance of something into other is possible. For example, if we say that cognisance of the serpent into rope has taken place, (svavachovyāghātāt) our own statement becomes self-contradictory, as the moment we recognised rope as a serpent, it was the serpent itself. The next time, when we recognised rope as rope, it was not the serpent by the rope.

Then, how to explain sat and asat-khyāti [right and wrong cognisance]?

सदसत्ख्यातिर्बाधाबाधात् ॥ ५६ ॥

sadasatkhyātirbādhābādhāt ॥ 56 ॥

(sadasat-khyātiḥ) The right cognisance [sat khyāti] and wrong cognisance [asat-khyāti] (bādha-abādhanāt) depends upon the interruption of connection and non-interruption of connection, respectively.

For example, when the wrong cognisance of the serpent into the rope takes place, the connection of the rope with the serpent is not interrupted. When the right cognisance of rope takes place, the connection of the serpent with the rope is interrupted.

Do words have the nature of sphoṭa?

प्रतीत्यप्रतीतिभ्यां न स्फोटात्मकः शब्दः ॥ ५७ ॥

pratītyapratītibhyāṁ na sphoṭātmakaḥ śabdaḥ ॥ 57 ॥

Ascertainment of intended objects [meaning] through the concerned words is called sphoṭa. Since it is supposed that words are helpful in the ascertainment of objects [meaning] intended by them. So it is said that words have the nature of sphoṭa.

But the author says that the (na sphoṭātmakaḥ śabdaḥ) words do not have the nature of sphoṭa, (pratīti-apratītibhyām) as they may or may not help ascertain the intended object [meaning]. Sometimes, the words can help to ascertain the intended meaning and sometimes not.

.

The author maintains that sound is not eternal.

न शब्दनित्यत्वं कार्यताप्रतीतेः ॥ ५८ ॥

na śabdanityatvaṁ kāryatāpratīteḥ ॥ *58* ॥

(na śabda-nityatvam) The sound is not eternal (kāryatā pratīteḥ) as we know that they are produced.

Here, we may have an objection and can say that only the objects that pre-exist in Prakṛti in seed form are produced in creation. No new object can be produced. For example, only such trees are produced by the seed that pre-exists in them as information. The same argument may be applied to the eternity of sound.

पूर्व सिद्धसत्त्वस्याभिव्यक्तिर्दीपिनेव घटस्य ॥ ५९ ॥

pūrva siddhasattvasyābhivyaktirdīpeneva ghaṭasya ॥ *59* ॥

(pūrva-siddha-sattvasya) Similarly, the sounds pre-exist, and they (abhivyaktiḥ) are manifested by articulation (dīpena iva ghaṭasya) as a pot preexisting in darkness is manifested by the lamp.

The author refutes the above proposition.

सत्कार्यसिद्धान्तश्चेत्सिद्धसाधनम् ॥ ६० ॥

satkāryasiddhāntaśchetsiddhasādhanam ॥ *60* ॥

If you mean the satkārya principle, according to

which only the entities [things that pre-exit in their causal form] are produced. Then, everything will be eternal in its causal form, and this would support what has already been maintained.

The principle of advaita (oneness) holds true in the case of Brahman. Does the same principle apply to souls also? To this, the reply is as under:

नाद्वैतमात्मनो लिङ्गात्तद्भेदप्रतीतेः ॥ ६१ ॥

nādvaitamātmano liṅgāttadbhedapratīteḥ ॥ 61 ॥

(na-advaitam-ātmanaḥ) Non-duality of the soul is not possible, (liṅgāt-tad-bheda-pratiteḥ) for differences in the souls are known through signs of old age, death, birth, pain and pleasures. Had there been one soul, all bodies would have experienced old age, death, and birth together simultaneously.

Now the question arises, is there advaita (oneness) in respect of souls and material body? In other words, can we say that body and soul, or mind and soul, are one? The reply is given in the next sūtra.

नानात्मनापि प्रत्यक्षबाधात् ॥ ६२ ॥

nānātmanāpi pratyakṣabādhāt ॥ 62 ॥

(anātmanā api na) The principle of advaita (oneness) does not apply in the case of the soul and the material body or mind, (pratyakṣa-bādhāt) because this is disapproved by sensory perception. For example, we can easily know that material objects like body, pot, clothes are lifeless.

Can both soul and matter together make advaita (oneness)?

नोभाभ्यां तेनैव ॥ ६३ ॥

nobhābhyāṁ tenaiva ॥ *63* ॥

(ubhābhyām) Both—soul and matter together (na) cannot make advaita (oneness), (tenaiva) because of the same reason [disapproval by sensory perception]. The soul is not matter; matter is not soul, so both cannot make one thing. The soul is bhoktā [experiencer], and the matter [body] is bhogya [worthy of being experienced], so experiencer and experienced cannot be one and the same thing.

If souls are many and the matter is different from the soul, what will be the significance of sentences like

'आत्मैवेदं सर्वम्'

'*ātmaivedaṃ sarvam*'

[Apparent Meaning] Soul is everything.

अन्य परत्वमविवेकानां तत्र ॥ ६४ ॥

anya paratvamavivekānāṁ tatra ॥ *64* ॥

The above sentences are actually intended to support dvaita, but apparently appear to support advaita. (anya-paratvam) So, another sense (tatra) in them [advaita] appears to (avivekānām) those who are aviveki [not able to discriminate between intended sense and apparent sense].

The intended meaning of 'आत्मैवेदं सर्वम्' '*ātmaivedaṃ sarvam*' is as under:

[Intended Meaning] The soul is everything in this body, identify its true nature to attain mokṣa.

नात्माविद्या नोभयं जगदुपादानकारणं निःसंगत्वात् ॥ ६५ ॥

nātmavidyā nobhayaṃ jagadupādānakāraṇaṃ niḥsaṅgatvāt ॥

(nātmā-avidyā) Neither the soul, nor avidyā [incorrect understanding or sense of permanence into transient], (na-ubhayam) nor both can be (jagat-upādānakāraṇam) the material cause of the world, (niḥsaṅgatvāt) because of non-altering nature of soul or avidyā.

What is difference between Paramātmā (Brahman) and Ātmā?

नैकस्यानन्दचिद्रूपत्वे द्वयोर्भेदात् ॥ ६६ ॥

naikasyānandachidrūpatve dvayorbhedāt ॥ *66* ॥

(dvayoḥ bhedāt) There is a difference between the two—Paramātmā [Brahman] and Ātmā [soul]. Brahman or Paramātmā is both All-bliss and All-knowing. (naikasya ānanda-chidrūpatve) But another Ātmā is not all bliss and all-knowing. The soul may experience pain and be ignorant.

In Vedic texts, sometimes blissfulness is also attributed to the ātmā. How do you justify it?

दुःखनिवृत्तेर्गौणः ॥ ६७ ॥

duḥkhanivṛttergauṇaḥ ॥ *67* ॥

Blissfulness is the innate [primary] attribute of the Brahman and not that of the soul. It is attributed to the soul (gauṇaḥ) relatively in the sense of (duḥkha-nivṛtteḥ) cessation of pain. The soul experiences bliss only in the state of mokṣa.

Why do we not accept that the state of mokṣa is blissful and a soul ultimately attains the same? All souls cannot attain mokṣa automatically. For mokṣa, a soul has to undergo a lot of penances.

विमुक्तिप्रशंसा मन्दानाम् ॥ ६८ ॥

vimuktiprasaṁsā mandānām ॥ 68 ॥

(vimukti-prasaṁsā) So, praise of mokṣa is done in the Vedic texts (mandānām) to inspire the thick-headed.

Is mind all-pervading or limited?

न व्यापकत्वं मनसः करणत्वादिन्द्रियत्वाद्वा ॥ ६९ ॥

na vyāpakatvaṁ manasaḥ karaṇatvādindriyatvādvā ॥ 69 ॥

(manasaḥ na vyāpakatvam) Mind is not all-pervading, (karaṇatvāt) because it is an instrument (vā) or (indriyatvāt) an internal sense-organ.

सक्रियत्वाद्गति श्रुतेः ॥ ७० ॥

sakriyatvādgati śruteḥ ॥ 70 ॥

The mind is not all-pervading (sakriya-tvāt) because it has motion, and there are also (śruteḥ) Vedic texts that mention the (gatiḥ) motion of the mind.

The mind is atomic, so is it eternal or not?

न निर्भागत्वं तद्योगाङ्घटवत् ॥ ७१ ॥

na nirbhāgatvaṁ tadyogāṅghaṭavat ॥ 71 ॥

Mind is composed [product] of Prakṛti; so, (nirbhāgatvam) it is not without composition. (tadyogāt) Being composed of matter like pot and other material things, (na) it is not eternal. An eternal thing has to be without any composition.

प्रकृतिपुरुषयोरन्यत्सर्वमनित्यम् ॥ ७२ ॥

Prakṛtipuruṣayoranyatsarvamanityam ॥ 72 ॥

(sarvam) Everything in this visible world (anyat) except (Prakṛti-puruṣayoḥ) Prakṛti [matter in its causal form] and Puruṣa [soul] (antiyam) is uneternal.

Why are Prakṛti and Puruṣa eternal?

न भागलाभो भोगिनो निर्भागत्वश्रुते: ॥ ७३ ॥

na bhāgalābho bhoginaṁ nirbhāgatvaśruteḥ ॥ 73 ॥

(bhoginaḥ) Bhoktā [experiencer] Puruṣa [soul] and bhogya [experienced] Prakṛti [matter] (na bhāgalābhaḥ) are not composed [product] of any other thing, (śruteḥ) Vedic texts also (nirbhāgatvam) describe them without composition.

Śvetāśvatara Upaniṣad (4.10) also describes that the products of Prakṛti permeate the whole world. Indirectly, it says that Prakṛti is without composition [not the product of any other element]. The verse goes like this:

मायां तु प्रकृतिं विद्यान् मायिनं तु महेश्वरम् ।
तस्यावयवभूतैस्तु व्याप्तं सर्वमिदं जगत् ।।

māyāṁ tu Prakṛtiṁ vidyān māyinaṁ tu maheśvaram,
tasyāvayavabhūtaistu vyāptaṁ sarvamidaṁ jagat.

[Meaning] Prakṛti is māyā, and Brahman is the controller of Prakṛti. The whole world is permeated by the products of Prakṛti.

At another place in the *Śvetāśvatara Up.* (6.19), it is said that the soul is not the product of anything. The verse is quoted below:

निष्कलं निष्क्रियं शान्तं निरवद्यं निरञ्जनम् ।

niṣkalaṁ niṣkriyaṁ śāntaṁ niravadyaṁ nirañjanam.

[Meaning] The soul is (niṣkalam) not the product of anything. (niṣkriyam) It does not move itself [because it moves in the company of mind or subtle body]. (śāntam) It does not waver. (nirvadyam) It is blameless and (nirañjanam) devoid of passions or emotions.

What is the sign of Mokṣa? Some may say that manifestation of bliss is the sign of mokṣa. The author refutes it.

नानन्दाभिव्यक्तिर्मुक्तिर्निर्धर्मत्वात् ॥ ७४ ॥

nānandābhivyaktirmuktirnirdharmatvāt ॥ 74 ॥

(ānandābhivyaktiḥ) Manifestation of bliss (na muktiḥ) is not mokṣa (nir dharmatvāt) because the soul is devoid of any property.

न विशेषगुणोच्छित्तिस्तद्वत् ॥ ७५ ॥

na viśeṣaguṇochchhittistadvat ॥ 75 ॥

(tadvat) Likewise, (viśeṣa-guṇa-uchchhitiḥ) the elimination of specific qualities of the soul (na) is also not mokṣa.

न विशेषगतिर्निष्क्रियस्य ॥ ७६ ॥

na viśeṣagatirniṣkriyasya ॥ 76 ॥

(na) Neither (viśeṣa-gatiḥ) soul's reaching to a particular place is mokṣa, (niṣkriyasya) as it is motionless. It can move with the subtle body only.

नाकारोपरागोच्छित्तिः क्षणिकत्वादिदोषात् ॥ ७७ ॥

nākāro parāgochchhittiḥ kṣaṇikatvādidoṣāt ॥ 77 ॥

(na) Nor can we say that (ākāroparāgochchhittiḥ) the elimination of the influence of the objects of the external world is mokṣa, (kṣaṇikatvādidoṣāt) as the influence of the objects of the external world on the soul is momentary and not permanent. At one moment, the soul is influenced by some external objects; at another moment, it will get rid of the influence and be called liberated. At another moment, it will be influenced by some other object and be called bonded. Thus, the mokṣa will become a ridiculous concept.

न सर्वोच्छित्तिरपुरुषार्थत्वादिदोषात् ॥ ७८ ॥

na sarvochchhittira puruṣārthatvādidoṣāt ॥ 78 ॥

(na) Nor the (sarvochchhittiḥ) entire destruction of the soul is mokṣa. (apuruṣārthatva-ādi doṣāt) If the soul is eliminated, who will get mokṣa? The very concept of mokṣa will become useless, as the mokṣa will no longer be the prime objective of the soul.

एवं शून्यमपि ॥ ७९ ॥

ēvaṁ śūnyamapi ॥ 79 ॥

(evam) Similarly, (śūnyam api) voidness [the destruction of bhūtākāśa, i.e. elemental space or the whole universe is not mokṣa because the soul's objective cannot be fulfilled either by the destruction of the soul or the annihilation of this universe.

संयोगाश्च वियोगान्ता इति न देशादिलाभोऽपि ॥ ८० ॥

saṁyogāścha viyogāntā iti na deśādilābho'pi ॥ 80 ॥

(deśādilābhaḥ api) Acquisition of material means like land, property, and others are (na) not mokṣa (sañyogāścha viyogāntāḥ) since conjunctions lead to disjunctions [separation].

न भागियोगो भागस्य ॥ ८१ ॥

na bhāgiyogo bhāgasya ॥ 81 ॥

(yagaḥ) The connection (bhāgasya) of part [soul] with (bhāgi) the body [supreme soul] (na) is also not mokṣa.

Generally, it is thought that the soul is part of

Brahman, so its connection with Brahman is mokṣa. Maharṣi Kapila sets this notion aside in the present sūtra.

नाणिमादियोगोप्यवश्यंभावित्वात्तदुच्छित्तेरितरयोगवत् ॥ ८२ ॥

nāṇimādiyogopyavaśyambhāvitvāttad-uchchhitter-itara-yogavat.

(aṇimādi yogo'pi) Attainment of divine powers like Aṇimā [reduction of the body to the level of the atom], Laghimā [becoming light], Mahimā [becoming very large], Prāpti [access to all places, even touching the moon while sitting on the surface of the earth], Garimā [becoming very heavy], Prakāmya [power of entering everything at will, even into the earth like that of waters], Vaśitva [control over all material things and other living beings including gross bhūtas], Īśitva [power of creation and destruction of all material objects] and Yatrakāmāvsāyitva [Satyasaṅkalpatā, i.e. instant materialisation of desires] (na) is not mokṣa, because they are not going to stay permanently, (avaśyambhāvitvāt uchchhitteḥ) their loss is inevitable (itara-yoga-vat) like other powers.

नेन्द्रादिपदयोगोऽपि तद्वत् ॥ ८३ ॥

nendrādipadayogo'pi tadvat ॥ 83 ॥

(tadvat) Similarly, (yogaḥ) attaining (indrādipada- api) the post and position of Indra and others is (na) not mokṣa.

Note: From here onward, 32 ślokas are interpolated, as they are out of the context of mokṣa, so I have deleted them.

Maharṣi Kapila has negated all the definitions of mokṣa cited above. Now, what is mokṣa? is explained hereunder:

समाधिसुषुप्तिमोक्षेषु ब्रह्मरूपता ॥ ८४ ॥

samādhisuṣuptimokṣeṣu brahmarūpatā ॥ 84 ॥

(samādhi-suṣupti-mokṣeṣu) Like in asamprajñāta samādhi, profound sleep, a seeker, in mokṣa, loses his/her existence and (Brahmarūpatā) attains oneness with Brahman.

So, according to Maharṣi Kapila, mokṣa is attaining oneness with Brahman.

However, samādhi, profound sleep and mokṣa are not similar states. In mokṣa, samādhi and profound sleep, we have identical realisation. Mokṣa, in fact, is a state, and in samādhi and profound sleep, we realise like mokṣa. The difference between the three is explained in the next sūtra.

द्वयोः सबीजमन्यत्रतद्धतिः ॥ ८५ ॥

dvayoḥ sabījamanyatra taddhatiḥ ॥ 85 ॥

(dvayoḥ) In asamprajñāt samādhi and profound sleep, (sabījam) the soul has the seed of sanskāra, (anyatra) but in mokṣa, (tad) the seed of sanskāra (hatiḥ) is completely erased or lost.

Note: Sanskāra acts as the seed for the next life. So long as the sanskāras of the external world or aham persist, there is no possibility of mokṣa. In asamprajñāt samādhi and profound sleep, the mind is not completely free from the sanskāras.

One may question that samādhi and profound sleep are evident, but what is the evidence of mokṣa? The reply is given by Āchārya as under:

द्वयोरिव त्रयस्यापि दृष्टत्वान्नतु द्वौ ॥ ८६ ॥

dvayoriva trayasyāpi dṛṣṭatvān-natu dvau ॥ 86 ॥

(na tu dvau) But not those two only [samādhi and profound sleep] evident, (trayasya api) the third one [mokṣa] is also (dṛṣṭtvā) evident, (dvayoriva) as are the two.

Samādhi and profound sleep are visible, but the third one [mokṣa] is the subject of realisation. The seers who had self-realisation had realised this state also.

वासनया नार्थख्यापनं दोषयोगेऽपि न निमित्तस्य प्रधानबाधकत्वम् ॥ ८७ ॥

vāsanayā nārthakhyāpanaṁ doṣayoge'pi na nimittasya
pradhāna-bādhakatvam ॥ 87 ॥

(vāsanayā) The sanskāras of the external world (na) do not help (arthakhyāpanam) in the awareness of the external world (doṣayoge) when interrupted by sleep because the sanskāras (nimittasya) causing awareness of (na) cannot (pradhāna-bādhakatva) stop sleep.

Note: Likewise, in samādhi, strong vairāgya [asceticism] interrupts the sanskāras of the external world.

As per the third chapter, the sanskāra of 'aham' helps the Jīvana Mukta [living liberated] person to sustain his body. Here, one may have a question: the previous sanskāras of Jīvana Mukta are exhausted, and new sanskāras are not accumulating due to self-realisation; in this condition, how can a Jīvana Mukta person experience the material body? The answer is given as:

एकः संस्कारः क्रियानिर्वर्तको न तु प्रतिक्रियं संस्कारभेदाः बहुकल्पनाप्रसक्तेः ॥ ८८ ॥

ēkaḥ saṁskāraḥ kriyānirvartako na tu pratikriyaṁ

saṁskārabhedāḥ bahukalpanāprasakteḥ || 88 ||

(ekaḥ sanskāraḥ) A single sanskāra of 'aham' suffices (kriyānivartakaḥ) to generate body for the bhoga (experience] of Jīvana Mukta till it last. (pratikriyam) For repeated [different] bhogas, (sanskārabhedāḥ) different sanskāras are (na tu) not required, (bahukalpanāprasakteḥ) otherwise we may have a postulation of many sanskāras.

In like manner, in the case of the whirling of the potter's wheel, the sanskāra of motion is to be regarded as only one, continuing till the whirling of the wheel.

Here is doubt. Human beings have a body that helps them get information from the external world. The plants do not have information from the external world; so they do not seem to have a body. The answer is:

न बाह्यबुद्धिनियमो वृक्षगुल्मलतौषधिवनस्पतितृणवीरुधादीनामपि
भोक्तृभोगायतनत्वं पूर्ववत् ॥ ८९ ॥

na bāhyabuddhiniyamo vṛkṣagulmalatauṣadhivanaspati-
tṛṇavīrudhādīnāmapi bhoktṛbhogāyatanatvaṁ pūrvavat ||89

(na bāhya-buddhi-niyamaḥ) It is unnecessary for a living being to lack a body if it cannot receive information from the outside world. (vṛkṣa) Trees, (gulma) shrubs, (latā) climbers, (auṣadhi) herbs, (vanaspati) vegetation, (tṛṇa) grass, (vīrudhādinām api) creepers and others are also abodes of bhoga [experience] for bhoktā [experiencer], (pūrvavat) as before [as in the case of human beings and other living beings].

Just as the human body decays without the superintendence of a bhoktā [experiencer] soul, even in the same way, withering takes place in the bodies of trees and plants. There is also testimony of Vedic texts in this respect. The *Chhandogya Upaniṣad* (6.11.32) says:

अस्य यां शाखां जीवो जहात्यथ सा शुष्यति ।

asya yāṁ śākhāṁ jīvo jahātyatha sā śuṣyati.

[Meaning] That very branch of a tree withers which the soul forsakes.

स्मृतेश्च ॥ ९० ॥

smṛteścha ॥ 91 ॥

(smṛteścha) The fact that trees have bodies is evident from the testimony of Smṛtis.

For instance, the *Manusmṛti* (12.9) says:

शरीरजैः कर्मदोषैर्यातिस्थावरतां नरः ।
वाचिकैः पक्षिमृगतां मानसैरन्त्यजातिताम् ॥

śarīrajaiḥ karmadoṣairyātisthāvaratāṁ naraḥ,
vācikaiḥ pakṣimṛgatāṁ mānasairantyajātitām.

[Meaning] In consequence of (many) unethical and immoral acts committed with its body, a soul gets the body of plants and trees, in consequence, unethical and immoral acts committed by speech, a bird, or an animal, and as a result of unethical and immoral acts committed by mind or thought, a soul is reborn in the bodies of illiterate and labourer human beings.

Since plants and trees have bodies, they should be able to pursue the acts of dharma and adharma.

न देहमात्रतः कर्माधिकारित्वं वैशिष्ट्यश्रुतेः ॥ ९२ ॥

na dehamātrataḥ karmādhikāritvaṁ vaiśiṣṭyaśruteḥ ॥ 92 ॥

Acts of dharma and adharma (na) cannot be pursued

(dehamātrataḥ) because of the body alone. (śruteḥ) According to the Vedic texts, (vaiśiṣṭya) only a human body [which has attained distinction among the bodies of all species] (karmādhikāritvam) is qualified to do new actions.

Note: Only the human species is called both karma-yonī [qualified to do new acts] and bhoga-yonī [bound to reap the fruits of karmas done in the past lives]. Otherwise, all other species are called only bhoga-yonīs, where they can reap the fruits of karmas done by them in their past lives.

त्रिधा त्रयाणां व्यवस्था कर्मदेहोपभोगदेहोभयदेहाः ॥ ९३ ॥

tridhā trayāṇāṁ vyavasthā karmadehopabhogadehobhaya-
dehāḥ ॥ 93 ॥

Bodies of various species have been divided into three types according to their qualifications:

1. Karmadeha: Qualified for doing new acts. Such bodies are attained by enlightened souls, like yogīs and Ṛṣis. They have no kārmic sanskāras accompanying them from past lives, so they are not required to reap the fruits of karmas done by them in past lives.

2. Ubhayodeha: Qualified for doing new acts and reaping the fruits of karmas done in the past life. This type of body is attained by souls occupying human bodies. They are qualified to do the bhoga of karmas of their past lives and perform new actions in the current life.

3. Upabhoga-deha: Qualified only for reaping fruits of karmas done in the past lives. This body type is attained by souls occupying bodies of lower species of

birds, animals, insects, plants and trees. In lower species, the souls cannot do new actions. They reoccupy human bodies after the exhaustion of their past karmas' bhoga [fruits].

In the transit period, when the soul transits from the old body to the new and waits to occupy a new suitable body and environment according to its kārmic sanskāras, it remains without a body [house]. This bodyless soul is called Anuśayin [a soul in a sleeping state or state of darkness].

न किञ्चिदप्यनुशयिनः ॥ ९४ ॥

na kiñchidapyanuśayinaḥ ॥ 94 ॥

(anuśayinaḥ) Anuśayin [a soul in a sleeping state] (na) does not occupy (kiñchida) any of the above three bodies.

Here, one may raise the following question: if Buddhi [mind] is accepted as an eternal element, there will be no need for the soul. To this, the answer is given as follows:

न बुद्ध्यादिनित्यत्वमाश्रयविशेषेऽपि वह्निवत् ॥ ९५ ॥

na buddhyādinityatvamāśrayaviśeṣe'pi vahni-vat ॥ 95 ॥

Buddhi and mind are not eternal even if they are located in Brahman, as is the case with fire.

The author means to say that a thing never changes its basic nature. Buddhi or mind is the product of matter, so they will contain material nature even when residing in eternal Brahman, like fire is always hot by nature, even when it takes rise in sandalwood [which is cold by nature].

आश्रयासिद्धेश्च ॥ ९६ ॥

āśrayāsiddheścha ॥ 97 ॥

Moreover, if we do not accept the existence of the soul, (āśraya-asiddheḥ) mind will have no location to exist. As such, for the existence of Buddhi [mind], the existence of the soul is necessary.

Buddhi or mahat is the first product of Prakṛti followed by ahaṅkāra, mind, tanmātra, sense organs and others. This whole material expanse of Prakṛti is for the bhoga and apavarga of the soul. Based upon the soul, buddhi and others are functioning. If the existence of the soul is denied, everything will become useless.

Further proof of the existence of the soul is given.

योगसिद्धयोऽप्यौषधादिसिद्धिवन्नापलपनीयाः ॥ ९८ ॥

yogasiddhayo'pyauṣadhādisiddhivannāpalapanīyāḥ ॥ 98 ॥

The divine powers attained through yoga also prove the existence of the soul. Because any lifeless material thing cannot have such powers. (yogasiddhayaḥ api) The divine powers attained through yoga (na) cannot (apalapanīyāḥ) be denied (auṣadādisiddhi-vat) as the powers gained through auṣadhis (ayurvedic rasāyanas), mantra, tapas and others.

न भूतचैतन्यं प्रत्येकादृष्टेःसांहत्येऽपि च सांहत्येऽपि च ॥ ९९ ॥

na bhūta chaitanyaṁ pratyekādṛṣṭeḥ sāṁhatye'pi cha

sāṁhatye'pi cha ॥ 99॥

(bhūtachaitanyam) The life [chetanā] in Prakṛti [matter] is (na) not possible, (adṛṣṭeḥ) as the same has never been detected (pratyeka) in atoms of it. (sāṅhateye api cha) Nor does life [chetanā] rise from the compound of elements. It [chetanā or soul] exists independently of Prakṛti [matter or energy].

Sixth Chapter

In the sixth chapter existence of Ātmā [the soul] as an independant entity other than Prakṛti is established.

अस्त्यात्मा नास्तित्वसाधनाभावात् ॥ १ ॥

astyātmā nāstitvasādhanābhāvāt ॥ 1 ॥

(asti Ātmā) The soul exists, (nāstitva-sādhana-abhāvāt) because there is not proof of its non-existence.

देहादिव्यतिरिक्तोऽसौवैचित्र्यात् ॥ २ ॥

dehādivyatirikto'sau vaichitrayāt ॥ 2 ॥

(asau) The soul is (vyatiriktaḥ) different from the (dehādi) body, mind and others (vaichitrayāt) because of its specific qualities.

For example, the body and others are the means of bhoga [experience] and the soul is bhoktā [experiencer]. The body and others undergo changes, and the soul is changeless.

षष्ठीव्यपदेशादपि ॥ ३ ॥

ṣaṣṭhīvyapadeśādapi ॥ 3 ॥

The existence of the soul is proved (ṣaṣṭhī-vyapadeśāt api] on account of the use of genetive [possessive] case by the people.

For example, we generally say, 'This is my body', 'This is my hand', 'It comes to my mind' and so on. This shows that some other entity exists other than the body and hand that claims possession of the body and hand.

The genetive [possessive] case is mostly employed where the difference between possessed and possessor exists. However, there are also examples where the possessive case is used where there is no difference between the possessor and possessed, like the statues of stone. Here, there is no difference between statue and stone. In this case, one may raise a question about the statement of a possessive case like 'This is my body'; there is no difference between possessor [soul] and possessed [body]. So, the above statement also means that body and soul are one. To this, the following reply is given:

न शिलापुत्रवद्धर्मिग्राहकमानबाधात् ॥ ४ ॥

na śilāputravaddharmigrāhakamānabādhāt ॥ *4* ॥

(śilāputravad) The comparison of the possessive case of the body with the case of the statue is (na) not proper because (dharmī-grahaka-māna-bādhāt) when the true nature of possessor [soul] denoted by 'I', 'my' in the sentence 'This is my body', is identified, body [possessed] is excluded from the soul [possessor]. However, in the case of a statue, the statue is not excluded from the stone.

Having settled issue that soul is different from body, now the issue of the mokṣa of the soul is settled.

अत्यन्तदुःखनिवृत्त्या कृतकृत्यता ॥ ५ ॥

atyantaduḥkhanivṛttyā kṛtakṛtyatā ॥ *5* ॥

(atayanta-duḥkhanivṛttyā) Permanent cessation of pain leads to (kṛta-kṛtyatā) the mokṣa.

In mokṣa, both sensory pain and pleasure are alleviated. While defining mokṣa, it was not stated that cessation of sensory pleasure is mokṣa; why was it stated that cessation of sensory pain is mokṣa? The reply is as follows:

यथा दुःखात्क्लेशःपुरुषस्य न तथा सुखादभिलाषः ॥ ६ ॥

yathā duḥkhātkleśa: puruṣasya na tathā sukhādabhilāṣaḥ ॥ 6 ॥

(puruṣasya) Soul has (na) no (tathā) so much (abhilāṣaḥ) desire (sukhād) for sensory pleasure, (yathā) as it has (kleśaḥ) aversion (duḥkhāt) to sensory pain.

कुत्रापि कोऽपि सुखीति ॥ ७ ॥

kutrāpi ko'pi sukhīti ॥ 7 ॥

(ko'pi) Only a few are (sukhīti) seen happy (kutrāpi) somewhere.

तदपि दुःखशबलमिति दुःखपक्षे निःक्षिपन्ते विवेचकाः ॥ ८ ॥

tadapi duḥkhaśabalamiti duḥkhapakṣe niḥkṣipante vivechakāḥ.

Sensory pleasure is also mixed with sensory pain, so analysts reckon sensory pleasure as sensory pain.

सुखलाभाभावादपुरुषार्थत्वमिति चेन्नद्वैविध्यात् ॥ ९ ॥

sukhalābhābhāvādapuruṣārthatvamiti chenna dvaividhyāt ॥ 9 ॥

If you say that cessation of sensory pain is (apuruṣārthatvam) not soul's objective, (sukhalābhābhāvāt) unless there is acquisition of sensory pleasure, (chet na) then it is not so, (dvaividhyāt) because there are two types of pleasures—sensory and spiritual. In mokṣa, we do not have sensory pleasure, but spiritual bliss.

निर्गुणत्वमात्मनोऽसङ्गत्वादिश्रुतेः ॥ १० ॥

nirguṇatvamātmano'saṅgatvādiśruteḥ ॥ 10 ॥

In this sūtra, an objection has been raised. (nirguṇatvam ātmanaḥ] The soul is devoid of qualities like sukha [sensory pleasure], duḥkha [sensory pain], sattva, rajas, tamas and other guṇas, (asaṅgatvādi śruteḥ) since the Vedic texts have described the soul asaṅga [free from attachment]. For example, Bṛhadāraṇyaka Up. (4.3.16) says:

असंगोऽह्ययं पुरुषः निर्गुणः ।

asaṅgo'hyayaṃ puruṣaḥ nirguṇaḥ.

[Meaning] This soul is free from attachment and guṇas.

Then what is the meaning of cessation of pain. The Āchārya replies:

परधर्मत्वेऽपि तत्सिद्धिरविवेकात् ॥ ११ ॥

paradharmatve'pi tatsiddhiravivekāt ॥ *11* ॥

(paradharmatve) Although sensory pain and pleasure are the property of the body, (tatsiddhiḥ) they are experienced by the soul (avivekāt) because the soul identifies itself with the body.

Ātmā experiences sensory pain and pleasure because of aviveka [identifying itself with the body]. But what is the source of aviveka in Ātmā? The seer replies:

अनादिरविवेकोऽन्यथा दोषद्वयप्रसत्तेः ॥ १२ ॥

anādiraviveko'nyathā doṣadvayaprasakteḥ ॥ *12* ॥

(avivekaḥ) Aviveka [the soul's identifying itself with the body] (anādiḥ) is eternal; it stays with ātman as sanskāra during dissolution. If we do not accept aviveka eternal, (doṣa-dvaya-prasakteḥ) it will raise two objections. Firstly, if we think that aviveka may develop automatically, it may grow even during mokṣa, causing the immediate bondage of the liberated soul. Secondly, mokṣa will take place itself before the rise of aviveka.

If aviveka is eternal, it must be everlasting. To this, the reply is as under:

न नित्यः स्यादात्मवदन्यथानुच्छित्तिः ॥ १३ ॥

na nityaḥ syādātmavadanyathānuchchhittiḥ ॥ *13* ॥

Aviveka is (na syāt) not (nityaḥ) an eternal entity (ātmavat) like the soul (anyathā); otherwise, it would be (anuchchhittiḥ) everlasting.

In fact, Aviveka is a vṛtti [state] of mind that helps the soul identify itself with the body. It can be withdrawn like other vṛttis [states of mind].

How is aviveka as the cause of Soul's bondage annihilated? The Āchārya replies:

प्रतिनियतकारणनाश्यत्वमस्य ध्वान्तवत् ॥ १४ ॥

pratiniyatakāraṇanāśyatvamasya dhvāntavat ॥ *14* ॥

(asya) The aviveka is (nāśyatvam) annihilated by its (pratiniyat-kāraṇam) fixed opposite cause Viveka [Soul's identification of its true nature], (dhvāntavat) like darkness is destroyed by its fixed opposite cause, light.

अत्रापि प्रतिनियमो ऽन्वयव्यतिरेकात् ॥ १५ ॥

atrāpi pratiniyamo 'nvayavyatirekāt ॥ *15* ॥

(atra) In the annihilation of aviveka (pratiniyamaḥ) by its fixed opposite cause, Viveka, (anvaya-vyatirekāt) follows the principle of 'Anvaya-vyatireka' where the presence of viveka is marked by the absence of aviveka, and vice versa. Just like the presence of light is marked by the absence of darkness and vice versa.

Is there any other cause of bondage?

प्रकारान्तरासंभवादविवेक एव बन्धः ॥ १६ ॥

prakārāntarāsaṁbhavādaviveka eva bandhaḥ ॥ 16 ॥

(asambhavāt) There is no possibility of bondage (prakārāntara) in any other way, so, (aviveka) aviveka (eva) alone is the cause of (bandhaḥ) bondage.

न मुक्तस्य पुनर्बन्धयोगोऽप्यनावृत्तिश्रुतेः ॥ १७ ॥

na muktasya punarbandhayogo'pyanāvṛttiśruteḥ ॥ 17 ॥

There is (na) no chance of (punarbandha-yogaḥ) renewed bondage to the (muktasya) liberated person in the current creation cycle (anāvṛttiśruteḥ) because there is a Vedic text for its non-recurrence. Once liberated, it will take birth in the subsequent creation cycle.

अपुरुषार्थत्वमन्यथा ॥ १८ ॥

apuruṣārthatvamanyathā ॥ 18 ॥

(anyathā) Had the liberated persons been in renewed bondage, (apuruṣārthatvam) liberation would have ceased to be the supreme objective of the soul.

अविशेषापत्तिरुभयोः ॥ १९ ॥

aviśeṣāpattirubhayoḥ ॥ 19 ॥

(ubhayoḥ) And both liberated and bonded souls would be (aviśeṣāpattiḥ) alike. That is, there would be no difference between bondage and liberation.

If liberation and bondage are two different states, why is the soul considered eternal in Sāṅkhya (1.19)? An eternal soul cannot have two different states. How would you justify the difference between bondage and liberation?

मुक्तिरन्तरायध्वस्तेर्न परः ॥ २० ॥

muktirantarāyadhvasterna paraḥ ॥ 20 ॥

(muktiḥ) Mokṣa is (na) nothing (paraḥ) else but the (antarāya-dhvasteḥ) removal of obstacle [i.e. aviveka] to Soul's recognition of its true nature].

Previously, cessation of three types of pain was called Puruṣārtha [mokṣa], now you are saying that cessation of an obstacle to the Soul's recognition of its true nature is mokṣa. Is there no contradiction?

तत्राप्यविरोधः ॥ २१ ॥

tatrāpyavirodhaḥ ॥ 21 ॥

(tatra api avirodhaḥ) There is no contradiction in saying cessation of pain or cessation of obstacle. Aviveka is an obstacle that is the cause of pain. So, cessation of cause or cessation of effect is one and the same thing.

Suppose liberation is merely the removal of the obstacle of aviveka. In that case, it should be accomplished through the mere hearing [śravaṇa] of knowledge of Viveka [recognition of the soul's true nature].

अधिकारित्रैविध्यान्न नियमः ॥ २२ ॥

adhikāritraividhyānna niyamaḥ ॥ 22 ॥

(adhikāri-traividhyāt) Seekers of mokṣa can be categorised into three types as per their qualifications, viz. manda [weak], madhyama [mediocre] and tivra [prominent]. Prominent [having the sanskāra of viveka from past lives] is liberated as a consequence of mere hearing [śravana], the mediocre as a consequence of śravana [hearing] and thinking [manana] and the weak by practising all three, i.e. hearing, thinking and meditation [nidhidhyāsana]. (na niyamaḥ) So, there is no such rule that every seeker will attain mokṣa on account of hearing.

What should others unable to realise Viveka on hearing, do to strengthen viveka?

दाढ्यार्थमुत्तरेषाम् ॥ २३ ॥

dārḍhyārtham uttareṣām ॥ 23 ॥

(dārḍhyārtham) To strengthen viveka, (uttareṣām) they should follow the practice of the other two — manana [thinking] and nidhidhyāsana [meditation].

Is there any particular Āsana for meditation?

स्थिरसुखमासनमिति न नियमः ॥ २४ ॥

sthirasukhamāsanamiti na niyamaḥ ॥ 24 ॥

(sthira-sukham-āsanam) Any posture that is steady and comfortable will suffice. There is (na) no (niyamaḥ) rule of a particular posture.

What is meditation?

ध्यानं निर्विषयं मनः ॥ २५ ॥

dhyānaṁ nirviṣayaṁ manaḥ ॥ 25 ॥

Meditation [fixed attention for a long time] is the mind without an object.

When the soul is unattached, what is the need for meditation?

उभयथाप्यविशेषश्चेन्नैवमुपरागनिरोधाद्विशेषः ॥ २६ ॥

ubhayathāpyaviśeṣaśchennaivamuparāganirodhādviśeṣaḥ ॥ 26

(chet) Should you say that (ubhayathā) whether one

meditates or not, in both cases (aviśeṣaḥ) the soul remains unaffected, (na evam) it is not correct? In meditation, (uparāga nirodhāt) pain is excluded, which persists otherwise. (viśeṣaḥ) This makes the state of meditation special compared to non-meditation.

निःसङ्गेऽप्युपरागोऽविवेकात् ॥ २७ ॥

niḥsaṅge'pyuparāgo'vivekāt ॥ 27 ॥

(niḥsaṅge api) Though the soul is unattached to guṇas, (uparāgaḥ), it experiences pain (avivekāt) due to aviveka.

What is the nature of pain?

जपास्फटिकयोरिव नोपरागः किंत्वभिमानः ॥ २८ ॥

japāsphaṭikayoriva noparāgaḥ kiṁ tvabhimānaḥ ॥ 28 ॥

(iva) Like the (japā-sphaṭikayoḥ) hibiscus flower, when it comes in contact with the crystal, it leaves the image of its red colour, and the crystal appears red without being coloured so. Similarly, due to aviveka, the soul (abhimānaḥ) feels pain in contact with the body and mind (uparāgaḥ na), although it does not have actual pain.

How this feeling of pain can be removed?

ध्यानधारणाभ्यासवैराग्यादिभिस्तनिरोधः ॥ २९ ॥

dhyānadhāraṇābhyāsavairāgyādibhistanirodhaḥ ॥ 29 ॥

(abhyāsa) By practising (dhyāna) meditation [fixed attention for a long time], concentration [fixed attention], and renunciation, a seeker can get rid of this feeling of pain.

लयविक्षेपयोर्व्यावृत्त्येत्याचार्याः ॥ ३० ॥

layavikṣepayorvyāvṛttyetyāchāryāḥ ॥ 30 ॥

(iti Āchāryaḥ) As per some Āchāryas of Sāṅkhya school, through meditation, all states of mind (laya-vikṣapayoḥ) known as laya [sleep] and vikṣepa [distraction state of mind] (vyāvṛttiḥ) are withdrawn and so the feeling of pain also withdrawn.

Note: There are four vikṣepa [distraction] states of mind—

1. Pramāṇa or cognition

2. Viparyaya or false cognition

3. Vikalpa or fiction and

4. Smṛti or memory

Is there any specific place required to attain perfection in meditation [dhyana]?

न स्थाननियमश्चित्तप्रसादात् ॥ ३१ ॥

na sthānaniyamaśchittaprasādāt ॥ 31 ॥

(na sthāna-niyamaḥ) No specific place is required, as perfection in meditation is attained by the (chitta-prasādāt) tranquillity of mind. So, any place conducive to the tranquillity of mind is perfect for meditation.

Here ends the discussion on mokṣa. Now, the source of buddhi, mind and others that help the soul in experiencing bhoga and mokṣa will be dealt with.

प्रकृतेराद्योपादानतान्येषां कार्यत्वश्रुतेः ॥ ३२ ॥

prakṛter ādyopādānatāny-eṣāṁ kāryatvaśruteḥ ॥ 32 ॥

(prakṛteḥ ādya upādanatāni) Prakṛti is the primary

material cause of all material things starting from mahat [buddhi] till five gross bhūtas because (anyeṣām) other material things are stated (kāryatva-śruteḥ) to be the products of Prakṛti by the Vedic texts. For instance Śvetāśvatara Up. (4.5) says:

अजामेकां लोहितशुक्लकृष्णां बह्वीः प्रजाः सृजमानां सरूपाः ।
अजो ह्येको जुषमाणोऽनुशेते जहात्येनां भुक्तभोगामजोऽन्यः ॥

ajāmekāṁ lohitaśuklakṛṣṇāṁ bahvīḥ prajāḥ sṛjamānāṁ sarūpāḥ,

ajo hyeko juṣamāṇo'nuśete jahātyenāṁ bhuktabhogāmajo'nyaḥ.

[Meaning] There is one (ajām) Prakṛti composed of (śukla) sattva (lohita) rajas and (kṛṣṇa) tamas guṇas, who is ever bringing forth all material forms. She alone exists embracing the whole material expanse; another unborn 'soul' abandons it in mokṣa, when all its bhogas [experiences] have been experienced.

Prakṛti is the primary cause of all material things because the Prakṛti is not the product of any cause. The soul is also not the product of any cause. Why do we not accept the soul as the primary material cause?

नित्यत्वेऽपि नात्मनो योग्यत्वाभावात् ॥ ३३ ॥

nityatve'pi nātmano yogyatvābhāvāt ॥ *33* ॥

(api) Though the (ātmanaḥ) soul is (nityatve) eternal, (yogyatā abhāvāt) it does not qualify for being the material cause.

Eternity is not the only qualification to be the material cause. A material cause should have guṇas [sattva, rajas and tamas] and qualify for attachment to others.

One may argue that the soul itself is a doer and experiencer irrespective of the contact of Prakṛti. It also qualifies as a material cause in the state of aviveka. The opinion of the author is as follows:

श्रुतिविरोधान्न कुतर्कापसदस्यात्मलाभः ॥ ३४ ॥

śrutivirodhānna kutarkāpasadasyātmalābhaḥ ॥ 34 ॥

(kutarka) These arguments are illogical and (śruti-virodhāt) contradictory to the Vedic texts. (kutarka-apasadasya) A person overwhelmed by illogical arguments (na) cannot experience (ātmalābhaḥ) self-realisation.

It is generally seen that all material things are the product of the Earth, so why do we consider Prakṛti as the material cause and not the earth?

पारम्पर्येऽपि प्रधानानुवृत्तिरणुवत् ॥ ३५ ॥

pāramparye'pi pradhānānuvṛttiraṇuvat ॥ 35 ॥

It is correct that the things in this visible world are caused by the earth or some other bhūta, but it is also a fact that this earth and other bhūtas are the products of different entity, so there is a chain of material cause and effect. (pāramaparye api) If we search the chain of material cause and effect, (pradhānānuvṛtti) it is repeated till mahat [buddhi]. However, there should be some end to this chain of cause and effect. This chain of material cause and effect ends with Prakṛti. Prakṛti is the final material cause of the mahat. From mahat onwards, all entities are both cause and effect. This means they are the effect [product] of some entity and cause to another entity. But Prakṛti is the end cause. Prakṛti is the micro-most state of the matter (aṇuvat) like that of a particle.

The prime material cause Prakṛti is composed of three guṇas, yet it is called all-pervading. Why?

सर्वत्र कार्यदर्शनाद्विभुत्वम् ॥ ३६ ॥

sarvatra kāryadarśanādvibhutvam ॥ 36 ॥

(vibhutva) Prakṛti is all-pervading (sarvatra-kārya-darśanāt) because its products are seen everywhere.

If Prakṛti is all-pervading, then it will be without motion. The author says, yes, it should be without motion.

गतियोगेऽप्याद्यकारणताहानिरणुवत् ॥ ३७ ॥

gatiyoge'pyādyakāraṇatāhāniraṇuvat ॥ 37 ॥

(gatiyoge api) If Prakṛti were subject to motion, it would be a product (aṇuvat) like atoms and (hāni) deprived of the character of (ādyakāraṇatā) ultimate material cause. So, Prakṛti has no motion. It is inactive energy.

Do the five gross bhūtas [element], the products of Prakṛti, inherit all the properties of Prakṛti, their material cause?

प्रसिद्धाधिक्यं प्रधानस्य न नियमः ॥ ३८ ॥

prasiddhādhikyaṁ pradhānasya na niyamaḥ ॥ 38 ॥

No, the five gross bhūtas do not inherit all the properties of their material cause, Prakṛti. Instead, (pradhānsya) Prakṛti has (ādhikyam) more properties than are (prasiddha) visible in its products. Like the ultimate cause, Prakṛti is eternal, while its products are not. So, there is (na) no (niyama) such rule that a product will inherit all the properties of its material cause.

Are Sattva, rajas and tamas the properties of Prakṛti or the constituents of Prakṛti?

सत्त्वादीनामतद्धर्मत्वं तद्रूपत्वात् ॥ ३९ ॥

sattvādīnāmataddharmatvaṁ tadrūpatvāt ॥ *39* ॥

(sattvādīnām) Sattva, rajas and tamas guṇas are (ataddharmatvam) not the properties of Prakṛti (tadrūpatvāt) rather the constituents of Prakṛti.

What is the purpose of creation?

अनुपभोगेऽपि पुमर्थं सृष्टिः प्रधानस्योष्ट्रकुङ्कुमवहनवत् ॥ ४० ॥

anupabhoge'pi pumarthaṁ sṛṣṭiḥ
pradhānasyoṣṭrakuṅkumavahanavat ॥ *40* ॥

(pradhānasya sṛṣṭiḥ) The creation of Prakṛti is (anupabhoge api) not for its own bhoga [enjoyment] but for the bhoga [enjoyment] of the soul, (uṣṭra-kuṁkum-vahan-vat) as the camel carries saffron not for itself but for his master.

What is the reason for diverse bodies of living beings?

कर्मवैचित्र्यात्सृष्टिवैचित्र्यम् ॥ ४१ ॥

karmavaichitrayātsṛṣṭivaichitrayam ॥ *41* ॥

(sṛṣṭi-vaichitryam) Diversity in the bodies of living beings is (karma-vaichtrayāt) in consequence of diversities of their kārmic sanskāras.

What is the difference between creation and decreation?

साम्यवैषम्याभ्यां कार्यद्वयम् ॥ ४२ ॥

sāmyavaiṣamyābhyāṁ kāryadvayam ॥ *42* ॥

(kāryadvayam) Decreation and creation are marked respectively (sāmya-vaiṣamyābyām) by the balanced and imbalanced state of sattva, rajas and tamas.

Creation of bodies for embodied souls [living beings] is a constant process by Prakṛti. Is there any time when Prakṛti stops its function for some souls?

विमुक्तबोधान्न सृष्टिः प्रधानस्य लोकवत् ॥ ४३ ॥

vimuktabodhānna sṛṣṭiḥ pradhānasya lokavat ॥ 43 ॥

(vimukta-bodhāt) When a liberated person realises Brahman (pradhānasya sṛṣṭiḥ na), Prakṛti ceases its function to create a body for the concerned liberated soul, (lokavat) as is seen in daily life. If somebody puts effort into releasing someone from prison, he/she abandons efforts when the concerned person is released.

नान्योपसर्पणेऽपि मुक्तोपभोगो निमित्ताभावात् ॥ ४४ ॥

nānyopasarpaṇe'pi muktopabhogo nimittābhāvāt ॥ 44 ॥

(api) However, Prakṛti (anya upasarpaṇe) continues to function [create bodies] as before for others who are not liberated; (na mukta-upabhogaḥ) only the liberated person becomes free from bhoga [reaping the fruits of his/her karmas], (nimittābhāvāt) because of the absence of cause [kārmika sanskāras] of bhoga.

पुरुषबहुत्वं व्यवस्थातः ॥ ४५ ॥

puruṣabahutvaṁ vyavasthātaḥ ॥ 45 ॥

(vyasthātaḥ) Because of the system mentioned above [Prakṛti ceases to function for liberated but continues to function for those who are not liberated], (puruṣa-bahutvam) the multiplicity of souls is proved. Had there been only one soul, all bodies would have been eliminated with the liberation of any one soul.

There is another argument: the soul is one, but it appears manifold due to its upādhis [adjuncts like liṅga śarīra consisting of mind etc.]. Here, we must understand the concept of upādhi. Upādhis [minds] are external adjuncts of the soul that delimit its conditions like all-pervadedness, etc. Upādhi is not inherent in the soul. Just as one universal space appears manifold in rooms, pots, etc., due to various upādhis [walls] of the concerned rooms and pots, if these walls are dismantled, all spaces of various rooms will merge with universal space. Similarly, the soul is one; you may call it Brahman, Ātman or Puruṣa, but it appears manifold due to many upādhis [liṅga śarīras consisting of buddhi, ahaṅkāra, mind, etc.]. So, one may conjecture that the system of death, birth [in bondage] and liberation is accomplished due to various upādhis [minds that are adjuncts of the soul]. The author replies:

उपाधिश्चेत्तत्सिद्धौपुनर्द्वैतम् ॥ ४६ ॥

upādhiśchet tatsiddau punadvaitam ॥ *46* ॥

(upādhiś chet) If we postulate the existence of upādhi behind this system of death, birth and liberation, (tat-siddhau) and the existence of upādhi is proved, (punar dvaitam) then there will be duality [Ātman and Upādhi], upsetting the principle of non-duality.

If you consider upādhi to be unreal [illusory], the system of birth, death and liberation will become baseless, and the difference of upādhis cannot exist by which you account for the diversity of living beings. If you consider upādhi real, on that very account, duality will be established, leading to the existence of multiple souls due to multiple upādhis causing multiple living-beings.

द्वाभ्यामपि प्रमाणविरोधः ॥ ४७ ॥

dvābhyāmapi pramāṇavirodhaḥ ॥ 47 ॥

If you take upādhi for avidyā [aviveka] and (dvābhyām) acknowledge the existence of the soul and avidyā, (pramāṇa-virodhaḥ) the principle of non-duality will again be contradicted by your own postulation.

द्वाभ्यामप्यविरोधान्न पूर्वमुत्तरं च साधकाभावात् ॥ ४८ ॥

dvābhyāmapyavirodhānna pūrvamuttaraṁ cha sādhakābhāvāt ॥

Because (dvābhyām api) by admitting two—the soul and avidyā, (pūrvam na avirodhāt) first part of Sāṅkhya's dualistic theory of soul and body [product of Prakṛti] is not contradicted with neo-Vedāntic view of soul and avidyā. For example in the dualistic theory of Sāṅkhya soul is eternal, yet the body [product of Prakṛti] is non-eternal, similarly in neo-Vedantic theory of soul and avidyā supporting the principle of non-duality, the soul is eternal, and avidyā is non-eternal. (uttaram cha) However, so far as the second part of Sāṅkhya's theory, admitting the multiplicity of souls and eternity of Prakṛti as the ultimate material cause of the universe, and neo-Vedantic theory of non-duality advocating the existence of one soul alone is concerned, the postulation of non-duality and the upādhi based system of birth and death cannot be established (sādhaka-abhāvāt) for want of sufficient evidence.

If we say that the non-duality of the soul is established by soul's self-manifestation, the reply is as follows:

प्रकाशतस्तत्सिद्धौ कर्मकर्तृविरोधः ॥ ४९ ॥

prakāśatastatsiddhau karmakartṛvirodhaḥ ॥ *49* ॥

(prakaśataḥ tat siddhau) Suppose the non-duality of the soul is established by soul's self-manifestation, as the soul is of the nature of manifestation. In that case, the soul will become subject and object simultaneously, (karma-kartṛ-virodhaḥ) which would lead to another problem. No person can simultaneously be the subject and object in respect of an action.

Here, it may be pointed out that manifestation is not the property of the soul, through which the soul can prove its own existence. The soul is the manifestation itself. Sūtrakāra [author of the sūtras] sheds light on it—

जडव्यावृत्तो जडं प्रकाशयति चिद्रूपः ॥ ५० ॥

jaḍavyāvṛtto jaḍaṁ prakāśayati chidrūpaḥ ॥ *50* ॥

(jaḍa-vyāvṛttaḥ) Being distinct from the material body, (chidrūpaḥ) the soul, which is of the nature of chetanā, (prakāśayati) brings (jaḍam) the material body in light.

In accordance with the above proofs, the duality [multiplicity of souls] is established, then what becomes of the Vedic texts declaring non-duality?

न श्रुतिविरोधो रागिणां वैराग्याय तत्सिद्धेः ॥ ५१ ॥

na śrutivirodho rāgiṇāṁ vairāgyāya tatsiddheḥ ॥ *51* ॥

The resolution of duality [multiplicty of the souls] is (na śruti-virodhaḥ) not in contradiction with Vedic texts, apparently declaring non-duality of the soul, (tat-siddheḥ) because non-duality of the soul is declared (vairāgyāya) in order to promote detachment from sensory objects (rāgīṇām) in respect of those who are afflicted by carnal desires.

In fact, statements like 'the soul is everything', 'the soul is only the real thing, every other thing is unreal' are figurative emphasizing upon the importance of the soul to promote the feeling of vairāgya [detachment].

Mentions relating to the non-duality of the soul to promote detachment from worldly allurements should not be interpreted to mean 'falsehood of world'.

जगत्सत्यत्वमदुष्टकारणजन्यत्वाद्बाधकाभावात् ॥ ५२ ॥

jagatsatyatvamaduṣṭakāraṇajanyatvādbādhakābhāvāt ॥ *52* ॥

The world is reality [although changeable and perishable], because it is a product of real faultless material cause [Prakṛti] and because there is a dearth of evidence in Vedic texts disapproving its existence.

Note: Here, the word mithyā stands for changeability, not falsehood or unreal.

The author states that the world is the reality not merely in its existent state [at any given instant] but always.

प्रकारान्तरासंभवात्सदुत्पत्तिः ॥ ५३ ॥

prakārāntarāsaṁbhavātsadutpattiḥ ॥ *53* ॥

(prakārāntara-asaṁbhavāt) Since the other mode of production [production of non-existent and production from non-existent] is not possible, (sat-utpattiḥ) there can only be the production of what exists in its cause. Neither non-existent can be produced, nor anything from non-existent can be produced.

अहंकारः कर्ता न पुरुषः ॥ ५४ ॥

ahaṁkāraḥ kartā na puruṣaḥ ॥ 54 ॥

(puruṣaḥ) Soul alone [disembodied soul] is (na) neither kartā [doer] nor bhoktā [expriencer], (ahaṅkāraḥ) but the embodied soul accompanied by ahaṅkāra [the notion of I, my] (kartā) becomes the doer and experiencer.

चिदवसाना भुक्तिस्तत्कर्मार्जितत्वात् ॥ ५५ ॥

chidavasānā bhuktistatkarmārjitatvāt ॥ 55 ॥

(chidāvasanā) The soul is at the receiving end (bhuktiḥ) for reaping the fruits of karmas (tat-karma-arjitatvāt) because the soul earns those fruits through karmas done with the help of the body.

The soul is liable to reap the fruits of karmas done by the body under the superintendence of the soul.

Do liberated persons also return to mundane life?

चन्द्रादिलोकेऽप्यावृत्तिर्निमित्तसद्भावात् ॥ ५६ ॥

chandrādiloke'pyāvṛttirnimittasadbhāvāt ॥ 56 ॥

The liberated person reaches Brahmaloka [space of Brahma], yet there is (api) also (āvṛttiḥ) return from (chandrādiloke) Brahmaloka [the state of the mokṣa] to the mundane life in the subsequent creation cycle, (nimitta-sadbhāvāt) because of the existence of the cause of bondage [sanskāras of ahaṅkāra and aviveka] in liṅga śarīra in the seed form even in the state of mokṣa. During mokṣa, sanskāras of aham and aviveka remain in seed form. In the next creation cycle, they get a conducive atmosphere to grow [manifest] and cause the embodiment of the liberated soul.

Can mokṣa be attained as consequence of instructions of experts in this field?

लोकस्य नोपदेशात्सिद्धिःपूर्ववत् ॥ ५७ ॥

lokasya nopadeśātsiddhiḥ pūrvavat ॥ 57 ॥

(tatsiddhiḥ) Mokṣa (na) cannot be attained (upadeśāt) from the instructions of experts (lokasya) in this field. (pūrvavat) It can be attained by following the method of śravaṇa [hearing], manana [thinking or pondering over what is heard from the mouth of expert Guru], and nididhyāsana [meditation], as explained earlier.

How can one attain mokṣa?

पारम्पर्येण तत्सिद्धौ विमुक्तिश्रुतिः ॥ ५८ ॥

pāramparyeṇa tatsiddhau vimuktiśrutiḥ ॥ 58 ॥

(pāramparyeṇa) As per tradition, mokṣa occurs (tatsiddhau) after attaining viveka [self-realisation] and (vimukti-śruti) the same is confirmed by the Vedic texts.

As per Sāṅkhya, the soul is eternal and has no motion [because a moving thing cannot be eternal], but the Vedic texts speak of its motion; how do you explain it?

गतिश्रुतेश्च व्यापकत्वेऽप्युपाधियोगाद् भोगदेशकाललाभो व्योमवत् ॥ ५९ ॥

gatiśruteścha vyāpakatve'pyupādhiyogād bhogadeśakālalābho vyomavat ॥ 59 ॥

As Vedic texts talk about the soul's motion, it reaches the place and time of bhoga [experience] as a consequence of its connection with the upādhi or adjunct, as is all-pervading space is moved by its upādhis [pots] from one place to another place. Similarly, the soul moves with its upādhi [subtle or gross body]

Note: liṅga, i.e., the subtle body, is an adjunct of the

soul in its disembodied state; in the embodied state, both subtle and sthūla, i.e., the gross body, are the adjuncts of the soul. With the help of the gross body, the soul performs actions and reaps the fruits of its karmas. With the help of a subtle body, it goes to different species.

Should we say that the body only, without the superintendence of the soul, moves in its subtle or gross form? To this, the author answers:

अनधिष्ठितस्य पूतिभावप्रसङ्गान्न तत्सिद्धिः ॥ ६० ॥

anadhiṣṭhitasya pūtibhāvaprasaṅgānna tatsiddhiḥ ॥ *60* ॥

(anadhiṣṭhitasya) Without the superintendence of the soul, (pūtibhāvaprasaṅgāt) the body is subject to decay (na tat siddhiḥ), so the constitution of the body without a soul is not possible.

The constitution of the soul's body is initiated when the soul supervises the fusion of sperm and egg. If this fusion is suitably and successfully superintended, the zygote is formed based upon the kārmic sanskāras of the soul inherited by it from its past lives. These kārmic sanskāras in the zygote are transformed into DNA.

The success of the fusion of sperm and ovum depends upon the match of sanskāras of the superintending soul with the DNA [biological sanskāras] to be inherited from sperm and ovum. If the DNA of sperm and ovum does not match the DNA [sanskāras] of the superintending soul, this fusion is unsuccessful; if it matches, the fusion is successful.

There is one more option for the body's constitution without the soul. We can say that the body is constituted based upon the kārmic sanskāras of the soul, without the soul's superintendence. In this respect, the reply follows:

अदृष्टद्वारा चेदसम्बद्धस्य तदसम्भवाज्जलादिवदङ्कुरे ॥ ६१ ॥

adṛṣṭadvārā chedasambaddhasya tadasambhavāj jalādiva-
daṅkure ॥ *61* ॥

(chet) If you think that the body is constituted (adṛṣṭadvārā) based upon kārmic sanskāras of the soul (asambaddhasya) and there is no need for superintendence of the soul. In that case, (tat asambhavāt) the fusion of sperm and ovum will not be successful, as fusion of sperm and ovum is superintended by the soul (jalādivat aṅkure) like the growth of a sprout from seed is not successful without the connection of water with seed.

Note: Here, the word adṛṣṭa signifies 'sanskāras' of the soul.

Here, one more question arises. The soul is nirguṇa [free from sattva, rajas and tamas], so how can kārmic sanskāras [which are of sattva, rajas and tamas nature] belong to the soul? The answer is:

निर्गुणत्वात्तदसंभवादहंकारधर्मा ह्येते ॥ ६२ ॥

nirguṇatvāttadasambhavādahaṁkāradharmā hyete ॥ *62* ॥

(nirguṇatvāt) Since the soul is void of sattva, rajas and tamas qualities, (tat asambhavāt) so kārmic sanskāras either of sattva, rajas or tamas qualities cannot belong to the soul. (ete) These karmic sanskāras are, in fact, (ahaṅkāra-dharmāḥ) the property of ahaṅkara and, due to aviveka [identifying itself to buddhi, ahaṅkāra, mind and body] the soul owns them. In fact, buddhi and others are the means of the soul for its bhoga and due to aviveka, the soul identifies itself with them.

विशिष्टस्य जीवत्वमन्वयव्यतिरेकात् ॥ ६३ ॥

viśiṣṭasya jīvatvamanvayavyatirekāt ॥ 63 ॥

The soul, when connected with (viśiṣṭasya) body constituted of buddhi, ahaṅkāra, mind and others (jīvatvam) is called Jīva, (anvaya-vyatirekāt) otherwise pure soul.

Note: Anvaya-vyatireka means logical connection and disconnection. In the case of connection with the body, it is called Jīva; otherwise, [in the case of disconnection with the body] it is called the soul.

In other words, the embodied soul is called jīva, and the disembodied soul is called the pure soul.

Who is the doer of actions? The soul or God?

अहंकारकर्त्रधीना कार्यसिद्धिर्नेश्वराधीना प्रमाणाभावात् ॥ ६४ ॥

ahaṁkārakarṣadhīnā kāryasiddhirneśvarādhīnā pramāṇābhāvāt.

(ahaṅkāra-kartrādhīnā) The soul impressed by ahaṅkāra consisting of sanskāras (kāryasiddhiḥ) is the doer of actions and (na Īśvara] not Īśvara [God]. (pramāṇābhāvāt) There is no evidence in respect of the doership of God. However, the fruits of actions are under the control of Īśvara.

How is the Ahaṅkāra formed?

अदृष्टोद्भूतिवत् समानत्वम् ॥ ६५ ॥

adṛṣṭodbhūtivatsamānatvam ॥ 65 ॥

(adṛṣṭodbhūti-vat) Like the formation of karmic sanskāras, the formation of ahaṅkāra takes place (samānatvam) because there is a similarity in both. The ahaṅkāra of the soul, in fact, is formed of its karmic sanskāras.

What is caused by ahaṅkāra?

महतोऽन्यत् ॥ ६६ ॥

mahato'nyat ॥ 66 ॥

Except for mahat, everything else is caused by ahaṅkāra.

Viveka [discrimination between Prakṛti and soul] causes the cessation of all types of suffering, but the question is, what causes the relation of the Prakṛti and the soul?

कर्मनिमित्तः प्रकृतेः स्वस्वामिभावोऽप्यनादिर्बीजाङ्कुरवत् ॥ ६७ ॥

karmanimittaḥ prakṛteḥ svasvāmibhāvo'pyanādirbījāṅkuravat ॥

(prakṛteḥ sva-svāmibhāvaḥ) The relation of Prakṛti [experienced] and the soul [experiencer] is (karmanimittaḥ) caused by the kārmic sanskāras of the soul. This relation is (anādiḥ) endless (bījāṅkura-vat) like the seed and sprout.

अविवेकनिमित्तो वा पञ्चशिखः ॥ ६८ ॥

avivekanimittoṁ vā pañchaśikhaḥ ॥ 68 ॥

(aviveka-nimittaḥ vā) This relationship is also caused by the aviveka [soul's misidentifying itself with Prakṛti], (pañchaśikhaḥ) according to Āchārya Pañchaśikha.

लिङ्गशरीरनिमित्तक इति सनन्दनाचार्यः ॥ ६९ ॥

liṅgaśarīranimittaka iti sanandanāchāryaḥ ॥ 69 ॥

(iti Sanandanāchāryaḥ) According to Sanandana Āchārya, this relation is (liṅgaśarīra-nimittaka) occasioned by liṅgaśarīra [subtle body consisting of buddhi, ahaṅkāra, mind, five senses of perception and five senses of action].

After declaring the causes of the relation of the soul and Prakṛti [body], the Āchārya concludes it, declaring the objective of human life.

यद्वा तद्वा तदुच्छित्तिः पुरुषार्थस्तदुच्छित्तिः पुरुषार्थः ॥ ७० ॥

yadvā tadvā taduchchhittiḥ puruṣārthastaduchchhittiḥ
puruṣārthaḥ ॥ 70 ॥

According to the Āchārya, (yadvā tadvā) let it be any factor causing the relationship between the soul and body; (puruṣārthaḥ) the ultimate aim of human life is (taduchchhittiḥ) to eliminate this relationship.

॥ शास्त्रवाक्यार्थमुपसंहरति ॥

॥ śāstravākyārthamupasaṁharati ॥

The End